Anne Bamford

The Wow Factor
Global research compendium on the impact of the arts in education

Waxmann Münster / New York
München / Berlin

Bibliographic information published by Die Deutsche Bibliothek
Die Deutsche Bibliothek lists this publication in the
Deutsche Nationalbibliografie; detailed bibliographic data
are available in the Internet at http://dnb.ddb.de.

ISBN 978-3-8309-1617-8

Second edition, 2009

© Anne Bamford
Waxmann Verlag GmbH, 2006
Postfach 8603, D–48046 Münster

www.waxmann.com
info@waxmann.com

Cover Design: Christian Averbeck, Münster
Credits: Collection Projeto Presente
Children playing selfmade musical instruments free in nature where they
belong. This image shows one of the fun tours through "Morro da Pedreira"
(Environmental Protected Area) where the majority of the participants of
Projeto Presente live. After making and building the instruments using
pieces of garbage and natural materials there is nothing else better than to join
in and learn surrounded by the beauty of the countryside where they belong!
Typesetting: Stoddart Satz- und Layoutservice, Münster
Print: Druckerei Hubert & Co., Göttingen
Printed on age-resistant paper, DIN 6738

For Angus, Nina, Lachlan, Daniel and
all the other children in the world

Contents

Executive summary

The Wow Factor: Global research perspectives on the impact of the arts in education reports the findings of a UNESCO project, carried out in collaboration with the Australia Council for the Arts (The Council) and the International Federation of Arts Councils and Culture Agencies (IFACCA).

This executive summary briefly reviews our methods and findings. The first chapter of the book presents the background and the context for the report, including an overview of central issues.

The following chapters present an analysis of wide-ranging data collected regarding the extent and impact of arts-rich programmes on children and young people. Based on findings of a comprehensive survey conducted in 2004 and distributed to ministries of education and culture in the UNESCO membership countries (as well as by organisations of which these hold joint-membership, e.g. the *European Council*).

Acknowledging that a quantitative analysis can give but a partial understanding of the field, selected (representative) case studies of arts-rich programmes in over 35 countries have been used to exemplify issues.

The concluding chapter draws all the observations together for an overall sense of how the different arts-rich programmes can be characterized and compared, and includes recommendations about how – and to what extent – these may be improved upon in the future. The appendices at the end of this book present some of the data that was collected from each country, along with other relevant information such as details of the case studies that can be accessed online.

This book was written in consultation with an international team of experts on arts, education and social sciences. The international team was led by Professor Anne Bamford, Director of *The Engine Room, Wimbledon School of Art*, London. The international team investigated and evaluated worldwide standards of arts-rich education in order to understand the current trends and examples of best-practice models in the field.

Objectives

The commissioned research underpinning the findings in this book aimed to establish an international compendium on research demonstrating the impact of arts-rich programmes on the education of children and young people around the world.

In order to assess the impact of arts-rich programmes, the qualitative and quantitative information gathered from the extensive survey distributed in November 2004 was analysed. The following questions guided the analysis:

- How was the teaching of arts-rich programmes organised?
- Who are responsible for curriculum development and implementation of arts-rich programmes?
- What are the differences between the arts-rich programmes taught in the different countries?
- What determines the differences in content from country to country?
- What can be expected or recommended of arts-rich programmes in the future?

Methods

To address these broad research questions, the study focused on two main aspects:

1. Establishing a knowledge-base about the organisational frameworks and other conditions which regulate and structure the teaching of arts-rich programmes, and;
2. Application of qualitative and quantitative methods of analysis aimed at drawing conclusions about the role of arts-rich programmes in different countries.

Carrying out this research presented methodological challenges. On the one hand, it was necessary to use a relatively tight definition of the arts in order to gather overall comparable information about the extent, content, and impact of the different programmes. On the other hand, these definitions were often too narrow to capture the full extend of the programmes.

Arts education – as defined in the quantitative part of the project – aim:

- To pass on cultural heritage to young people, and;
- To enable them to create their own artistic language and to contribute to their global development (emotional and cognitive).

These definitions, as stated above, cannot stand alone. A work of art is an object that embodies a meaning. As Arthur Danto has said "nothing is an artwork without an interpretation that constitutes it as such"[1]. What is seen as art in one culture is not defined as such in another.

Given this, quantitative findings were interpreted through direct reference to qualitative case studies. Respondents of the survey were also provided with opportunities for citing examples of pertinent case studies and, in general, invited to give examples of programmes that fall outside the definition of arts employed in this study.

---

1   Danto quoted in Cynthia Freeland (2001) *Art Theory*, Oxford, Oxford University Press, p. 38.

Conclusions/Observations

Containing responses from over 40 countries and organizations, the book provides a global overview of the qualities of effective arts and education partnerships, including:

- Identifiable details of the impact of arts and education partnerships, and;
- Models of data collection and research methodology for investigating the impact of arts and education partnerships.

The overall findings of the research can be summarized as follows:

- The arts appear in the educational policy in almost every country in the world;
- There is a gulf between the 'lip service' given to arts education and the provisions provided within schools;
- The term 'arts education' is culture and context specific. The meaning of the term varies from country and country, with specific differences between economically developed and economically developing countries;
- In all countries – irrespective of their level of economic development – certain core subjects (e.g. drawing and music – but also painting and craft) were part of the curriculum;
- Economically developed countries tend to embrace new media (including film, photography, and digital art) in the curriculum;
- In economically developing countries greater emphasis is placed on culture specific arts (e.g. stilt walking in Barbados, and hair-styling in Senegal!);
- There is a difference between, what can be termed, *education in the arts* (e.g. teaching in fine arts, music, drama, crafts, etc.) and *education through the arts* (e.g. the use of arts as a pedagogical tool in other subjects, such as numeracy, literacy and technology);
- Arts education has impact on the child, the teaching and learning environment, and on the community;
- There is a need for more training for key providers at the coalface of the delivery-chain (e.g. teachers, artists, and other pedagogical staff);
- Quality arts education has distinct benefits for children's health and socio-cultural well-being;
- Benefits of arts-rich programmes are only tangible within high quality programmes (though no specific definition of what constituted such programmes were given, aspects of quality can be inferred from the data), and;
- Quality arts education tends to be characterised by a strong partnership between the schools and outside arts and community organisations. (In other words it is teachers, artists and the communities, which *together* share the responsibility for the delivery of the programmes).

Quality Education and Education for All: The role of the arts

> Before answering the survey, I would like to share with the coordinators the idea of Arts Education as a double dimension process - 'Education to the Arts' and 'Education by the Arts'. Thus it places the cultural coherence of the child at the heart of any educational strategy. Moreover, this vision increases the value of all the disciplines and processes that have always been used by the communities – according to their own culture – to mould children's identity through their emotional and cognitive predispositions. Hence the importance too of the social dimension of Arts Education which protects poor children from being marginalized from the educational system.
> 2004: Alioune Badiane, Ministry for Culture and Heritage, Senegal

A major finding of the research has been that there are well-researched and documented impacts of arts-rich education. As the quote from Senegal suggests, these fall under two distinct aspects, respectively: *Education in the arts* and *Education through the arts*.

The former can be described as being sustained and systematic learning in the skills, ways of thinking and presentation of each of the art forms – dancing, visual arts, music, drama – and produces impacts in terms of improved attitudes to school and learning, enhanced cultural identity and sense of personal satisfaction and well-being. Concurrently, education which uses creative and artistic pedagogies to teach all curricula, i.e. education through the arts – enhances overall academic attainment, reduces school disaffection and promotes positive cognitive transfer. These noted benefits are only accrued where there were provisions of quality programmes. Poor quality programmes, were seen to actively inhibit the benefits apparent in good quality programmes.

The aim of this book *The Wow Factor: Global research compendium on the impact of the arts in education* is to provide a significant body of analysed research that clearly documents the impacts of the arts within general education. By highlighting key examples of arts-rich education from around the world, it is intended that education and arts and cultural organisations will be able to use this book to compare the policies and practices within their own countries. The book also provides insight into high quality arts-rich education practices around the world that can serve as models of practice for teachers, artists and preservice educators working in a range of contexts.

The Wow Factor: Global research compendium on the impact of the arts in education is the first comprehensive analysis of research-based case studies from around the world. It makes a major contribution to scholarly inquiry into the field of arts education and will form a baseline of information for arts and education policy makers. The findings contained within this book *The Wow Factor: Global research compendium on the impact of the arts in education* will become the standard by which the quality of arts-rich education programmes will be determined. As a result of foregrounding the importance of the arts within general education it is hoped that the children of the world may soon receive their full educational and artistic entitlements.

Acknowledgements

This book is the direct result of an extensive research study commissioned by *UNESCO* and carried out in collaboration with the *Australia Council for the Arts* and the *International Federation of Arts Councils and Culture Agencies (IFACCA)*. This book would not have been possible without the funding and support provided by these three organisations. In particular, I would like to thank Teresa Wagner (UNESCO) for her vision and confidence to initiate this study and Christina Human (UNESCO) for her friendship, encouragement and help.

Without the tremendous intellectual and administrative backing provided by Sarah Gardner (IFACCA), Christopher Madden (IFACCA), Gillian Gardiner (Australia Council for the Arts) and Samira Hassan (Australia Council for the Arts) the broad scope and global nature of the research would not have been possible.

The critical provision offered by the arts education reference group (Michael Anderson, *University of Sydney*; Arnold Aprill, *Chicago Arts Partnerships in Education*; Gillian Gardiner, *Australia Council for the Arts*; Sarah Gardner, *International Federation of Arts Councils & Cultural Agencies*; Maureen O'Rourke, *Victorian Schools Innovation Commission*; Rod Parnall, *Victorian Department of Education and Training*; Robin Pascoe, *National Affiliation of Arts Educators*; Barbara Piscitelli, *Queensland University of Technology*; Simon Spain, *ArtPlay – City of Melbourne*; and, Tereza Wagner, UNESCO) was invaluable in ensuring a globally inclusive research design and a clearly delineated research base.

The design of the impact measurement surveys, quantitative data analysis and policy interpretation was the result of the expert advice given by Professor Matt Qvortrup, *The Robert Gordon University, Aberdeen* and I wish to thank him for his extensive commitment to the value of the arts within education and public policy.

Finally, I wish to acknowledge the substantial intellectual contribution made by all the survey respondents and providers of case studies. The openness with which policy makers, arts and education providers and practitioners were willing to share their research and experiences is testament to the collegiality of people from around the world who share the desire to make the arts a valued part of every child's education.

Preface

The Wow Factor: Global research compendium on the impact of the arts in education is the direct outcome of the *UNESCO* research project instigated to determine the impact of the arts within global education. This research was conducted in close collaboration with the *Australia Council for the Arts (The Council)* and the *International Federation of Arts Councils and Culture Agencies (IFACCA)*. The commissioned research underpinning this book aimed to collate and analyse international research demonstrating the impact (if any) of arts-rich programmes on the education of children and young people around the world.

In order to assess the impact of arts-rich programmes, the qualitative and quantitative information gathered was analysed to determine both overall global patterns and the way arts education is manifest in various countries. Examining all aspects of the policy and delivery of arts education, the research design began by investigating policy formation and curriculum development. This work was expanded through the detailed case studies that provided insight into the way these policies were enacted and the complexities of implementation of arts policy within the education sector. In a specific way, teaching and learning experiences were examined and issues such as teacher education, resources and limitations were highlighted. These factors were all considered within a framework of impact analysis that looked at the range of possible outcomes attributable to the arts and evidenced within detailed research studies. These effects were analysed in broad terms and ranged from the impacts on children and their learning, through impacts on perceptions of schools and community and ultimately to examining major impacts on intellectual, social, cultural and emotional well-being.

To address these research issues, the methodology chosen was predicated on the need to establish a knowledge-base about the organisational frameworks and other conditions which regulate and structure arts-rich education programmes. This was achieved through the application of mainly qualitative – but also quantitative – methods of analysis aimed at portraying the role and nature of arts-rich programmes in different countries.

Carrying out this research presented methodological challenges. On the one hand, it was necessary to use a relatively tight definition of the arts in order to gather overall information about the extent, content, and impact of the different programmes. On the other hand, these definitions were often too narrow to capture the full extend of the programmes. Within this research a broad definition of arts education was derived from the countries themselves. At the heart of all the definitions was the notion that an arts-rich model of education is endowed with provisions that serve to develop cultural heritage for young people and enable them to create their own artistic language and to contribute to their global development (emotional and cognitive).

These definitions cannot stand alone. What is seen as art in one culture is not defined as such in another. Given this, quantitative findings were interpreted through direct reference to qualitative case studies. Respondents were provided with opportunities for citing examples of pertinent case studies and, in general, invited to give examples of programmes that fall outside the more traditional definition of the arts.

By taking an open and inclusive approach to the consideration of arts-rich programmes within education, it was inevitable that questions could be asked about the types of programmes included as falling under the 'arts' banner. The research adopted an all-encompassing stance and did not attempt to make value judgements in relation to the merits of one art form over another. To this extent, the global research underpinning this book is testament to the diverse nature of the arts, yet within this multiplicity there are clear patterns in terms of quality provisions and the impact of these worthy programmes. This became the focus of the investigations.

The notion of "the wow factor" in education was a term that appeared in the qualitative comments contained within the surveys. This term was applied to mean the excitement and unexpected results that are difficult to be definitive about but have enormous impact on the teachers, artists, children and even communities where effective arts-rich education occurred. This term was used especially in relation to the children's artistic achievements. The chance that a child may make a new discovery, open their eyes visually, musically or through movement or drama for the first time, or produce some new and innovative response was the engine that powered many arts-rich education programmes. The unexpected 'wow factor' was a potent force that kept teachers, artists and children going in arts programmes despite often severe structural restrictions and difficulties associated with implementing art within particular context. This quote from an Australian artist/teacher describes the 'wow' factor – an impact which surpasses all impacts that may be more formally measured.

> I mean every school you do it at, you get a different style…every kid gets a different result and you can be enthusiastic about that and say, "WOW!" You know… I haven't seen that one before. I think the "wow" part is really important. One of the young teachers at one school was saying I sound just like you. I was saying, "Wow! Isn't that great …? Look at this… That is fantastic" Something like that and I thought, "Oh that is good, I've started another teacher teaching that way! It is good.

Chapter 1:
The arts are intrinsic

Introduction

The arts are an intrinsic part of the way humans operate in the world. There is evidence of the arts existing long before writing. Examples of art have been dated to pre-history as in the case of Australian Aboriginal art. People participate in the arts all over the world. All cultures sing, dance, recite, listen to tales, and put on performances. The arts have always been part of humanity's most vital concerns. All societies in the world engage actively in the art, and the arts are flourishing in modern society as we rely even more strongly upon their powers to get our message across.

Children are born aesthetically aware and they engage in the arts long before they can speak or write. If you watch young children at play, you will see them naturally communicating in artistic forms. Through the arts, youth construct meaning into a unified form. The arts emphasise how phenomena relate to each other. Holistic thinking and synthesis of ideas are fundamental to the future world. Given this view, the arts are fundamental to education as a means to provide students with the social and intellectual survival skills for the unforeseeable future.

If we look to the future, the growing importance of technology has led to a renaissance of interest in the arts. Contemporary aesthetic culture goes beyond what we would previously have termed 'art' or 'the arts'. As the impact of the arts on communication, technology and meaning making grows, our schools need to focus on arts-rich education that encourages critical thinking, problem solving, and reflection. The new reality is the critical and aesthetic realm of learning.

In our economy today, inventiveness, design and innovation are necessary for survival. Innovation demands that ideas are free flowing, which in turn requires that people be creatively and well educated. The young people of today will be the inventors of the new cultural patterns and social philosophies of tomorrow. They will need to be able to design the materials, conditions, and community to fit this new world. To achieve this, young people require sustained and sequential learning both within and through the arts.

Aligned with this, school reform will see the reconfiguration of schools to become less bound by the physical walls of the school and to increasingly become centres for connecting the child with a range of learning resources. The *Internet* has fundamentally changed the way we communicate and access knowledge. Students can more readily access information from galleries, museums and the broader educational community. In accordance with this trend, schools should extend the classroom boundaries to include art and cultural institutions and be flexible with time-tables and other structures to allow students to become immersed in their investigations.

The arts have an enormous part to play in the total experience of education that students receive. Students develop greatly in terms of risk-taking, confidence, and ownership of learning through involvement in the arts. The arts really are *involving*; they promote a sense of community through a shared sprit and encourage student motivation to learn. Through establishing connections with students, the arts offer something unique and intrinsic to the quality of education.

The arts directly contribute to positive self-perceptions and identity, vital to effective educational achievement and the pursuit of lifelong learning. The arts may assist in developing cultural awareness and the acceptance of self and others. Recent technological changes have also sparked considerable interest in the impact of the arts on students' learning in relation to emerging multimodal literacies.

Despite all these claimed benefits of the arts, education monitoring and issues of quality have still largely concentrated on achievement defined by quite limited notions of scientific, mathematical or technological thinking and the cultural dimension of education has been largely overlooked. This problem is compounded by a lack of sustained evidence of the benefits of arts-rich programmes on educational outcomes and definitional problems associated with the scope and nature of arts education as it is operates within schools.

Arts education involves

The term 'arts' is used to denote both instruction in the arts and artistic pedagogy used to instigate education. Richardson (1999: 25) defines the arts broadly and simply as being anything made by humans. Embedded within this definition are a number of assumptions. Richardson contends that the arts involve skills in creating something that is beautiful and/or moving in its form. He considers that the arts are constructed and sited within a cultural context. Definitions of the arts continue to be the subject of entire theories, and it is not the intention of this book to add to that extensive body of work. There is considerable questioning over whether a term such as the arts – with the 's' – is even an appropriate way to group disciplines whose paramount forms can be as diverse as portraiture, orchestra, ballet and Greek tragedy. Yet the dominant political and educational discourses widely use the term 'the arts' and embed within this term an assumption of unity underpinned by notions of culture, heritage, citizenship and creativity.

The first question the research underpinning this book asked was what was considered as being part of arts education within the context of particular countries, and the responses given yielded diverse, historical and yet contemporary attempts to define the parameters of the areas of study loosely termed 'the arts'. To accommodate this, an open and inclusive definition of the arts is adopted in this book. The following were the definitions used in the survey:

Glossary:

Arts education:
Arts education aims to pass on cultural heritage to young people, to enable them to create their own artistic language and to contribute to their global development (emotional and cognitive). Arts education therefore affects the child on both an academic and personal level.[2] There are two different approaches to Arts education:[3] Education in Art implies teaching the pupils the practices and principles of the various art disciplines, to stimulate their critical awareness and sensitiveness and to enable them to construct cultural identities. Education through art implies that art is seen as a vehicle for learning other subject content and a mean for teaching more general educational outcomes. Other subjects should hence be infused into arts education, especially social or cultural issues.

International compendium:
This is a collection of concise but detailed information on projects being undertaken in various countries around the world that include the arts as a vital part of innovation, learning and education. Will the compendium contain analysis, or meta-analysis, as well as information on what is being done?

Research:
This survey adopts a broad definition of research that includes any systematic investigation that attempts to explore the nature of the links between the arts and education. Research implies a gathering of data or material from a range of sources. It can include both traditional quantitative and qualitative methods and/or other informal or innovative approaches.

---

2   Victor Flussel, teacher and director of the CMFI (Centre de Formation pour Musiciens Intervenants) in Strasbourg.
3   From the document "Sharing the Vision: A National Framework for Arts Education in Canadian Schools" from the "National Symposium on Arts Education", a Canadian virtual symposium designed to be a communication center and interactive environment for arts education advocates, http://www.artsed.ca/Sharing_the_Vision.PDF

Impact:
Impact should be considered in its broadest sense. Impact describes the influence or effect of the project, research, policy or intervention. It can also include the impression created or the attitudes fostered by a project. Impact can include (but not be limited to) impact on policy, funding, formal education, informal education, curriculum, teachers, preservice teachers, children, artists, family and the community. It can include economic impact, social impact, cultural impact, spiritual impact, impact on identity and many other forms of impact.

Arts-rich programme:
Any educational plan, curriculum, educational practice, model of teaching and learning that involves the arts in a significant and substantial way and has a direct impact on the education of children.

Educational Contexts:
While primarily examining arts-rich activities that occur within schools, this survey considers that education is any form of systematic instruction that involves teaching and learning. It is acknowledged that education can occur in many locations and involves more than (but not excluding) the acquisition of numeracy and literacy. Under this definition of education, wisdom is engendered through skills, concepts, understandings and knowledge. Education is acknowledged to be a force in cultural development and to involve an understanding of tradition and contemporary and future society and practices.

Children and young people:
Any individual between the ages of 0 and 18 years of age.

Marginalised or 'at risk' (children) in terms of fulfilling their educational and artistic potential:
This refers to any children or young people for whom the established or regular patterns or offerings of formal education may be irrelevant, inappropriate and/or insignificant. Marginalised or 'at risk' children may feel unimportant, excluded and/or peripheral to education. They may perceive their exposure to education as being of no consequence and irrelevant.

Research Methodology:
Any system of processes and techniques used to investigate the way art and education can be studied or examined. Methodology can include, but should not be limited to, both traditional and non-traditional forms of data gathering and research inquiry. As part of the aim of the survey is to

reveal alternative and innovative arts research methodologies, we welcome inclusion of a range of approaches.

Appendix one contains a copy of the survey distributed to respondents.

Furthermore, the research attempted to not simply define arts education and explore its manifestations in practice, but to specifically examine what 'quality' arts education may be. 'Quality', is defined as being those arts education provisions that are of recognised high value and worth in terms of the skills, attitudes and performativity engendered. According to Pearsall (1998) quality implies something that has been achieved successfully. In the case of this book, quality is considered to exist as something that may include achievements, but goes beyond this to consider learning journeys, pathways, partnerships and recognition. Dewey (1934: 19) writes of quality as being characterised by a "heightened vitality." He further comments that quality signifies, "active and alert commerce with the world: at its height, it implies complete interpretation of self and the world of objects and events." Under this notion, quality is not a fixed disposition but rather as Kissick (1993: 27) notes, "quality is first and foremost an idea, its criteria are susceptible to influences from within a given society."

Starting point for the research

Global monitoring of educational standards has tended to focus on achievement in mathematics, literacy and scientific thinking. There are many anecdotal comments from children, teachers and parents that the arts have a major impact on schooling and learning. Yet sustained research on the global extent of this impact has been lacking. Concurrently, even if such monitoring of the artistic and cultural aspects of education were to occur, there does not exist a set of standards that could be universally agreed as being evident of quality provisions for art education. The qualities of consummate – or frankly even adequate – arts education have been poorly articulated in the literature. Yet highly successful arts-rich programmes are apparent in case studies of everyday practices of arts educators and artists working in a range of educational contexts. It was thus surmised that it may be possible to ascertain the salient qualities that inform principles and practice of effective arts-rich programmes around the world and the impact these successful programmes have. The combination of quantitative and qualitative methods applied in the global research on arts education was premised on the assumption that the elusive qualities apparent in effective arts-rich programmes in a range of contexts may be embedded in case studies of quality practice. Detailed examination of case studies from around the world, given a range of educational, economic and social contexts provides a source of knowledge and enlightenment and sheds light on their beliefs, knowledge and practices relating to arts education.

More broadly, arts education is a relatively neglected area for scholarly investigation. As Zimmerman (1994: 60) notes, there has been considerable neglect of research and practices related to arts teachers. This lack of research impacts negatively upon future directions in arts education. Additionally, Zimmerman (1994: 65) contends that teachers and artists need to be encouraged to find a voice and to be empowered to seek their own meaning and understandings as they engage in the practice of arts teaching. The results of the research have shown a clear gap between the espoused policy – that value the arts within education – and the actual 'in school' practices, that tend to fall significantly below the lofty aims existing in policy.

While substantial studies into the benefits of art education have been undertaken in the United States (USA), Canada, Australia, Finland, the United Kingdom (UK) and others, a comprehensive analysis had not been conducted of global research in arts education. Despite a range of studies indicating the benefits of the arts, the arts remain undervalued in many countries.

Organisation of the book

The overall structure of the book has been designed to look comprehensively at the state of arts education at the current point in time. The book utilises the data from the survey to present a wide-ranging picture of arts-rich education around the world. The rationale behind the original research is that it would be valuable to capture the current state-of-play in relation to arts education around the world and open this up for discussion so that at a local level teachers and artists they may be able to communicate aspects of their practice and beliefs, and at a national or state level ministries of education, arts and culture and educational and cultural agencies may be provided with inspiration for models of future arts-rich education. It is the contention of this book that through conversations, it is possible to differentiate the present from the future and to think how the present and the future are likely to differ. It is within a framework of future action and improvement that the research – and resulting book – is conceived.

Since, earlier attempts to enhance the quality of long-term, classroom based outcomes of arts-rich education programmes seem to have been largely ineffectual, the book provided an opportunity to gather large-scale data and yet allow for the presentation of case studies that encouraged the full involvement of teachers and artists. In presenting the meta-analysis, the book tries to combine the statistical data with the voice of the respondents so that equal attention is given to the 'big picture' as to the educational ecology surrounding arts-rich practices. It was equally significant to investigate what was happening in arts education today in a global and national level as it was to examine the ways teachers, artists and the community organise their formal and informal 'classrooms' and the scope of the programmes they provide. These localised case studies gave meaning to the complexity – and at times confusing – overall data and enabled the revelation of poignant aspects of on the ground operations that could be considered to be the qualities of effective arts-rich teaching and learning.

The vision of a future framework for quality arts-rich education is presupposed by the notion that a depth arts curriculum is possible and that the arts are both learnable and teachable. It is assumed in this book that new methods might nurture and cultivate critical reflection within the arts education community and that the setting of priorities and a research framework may assist in the development of arts education pedagogy.

Creative and interpretive models of inquiry provide a multiplicity of ways of knowing. Bearing this in mind, the book is essentially a perspective on people, things or events surrounding global arts education. It is not an absolute answer to a question nor does it attempt to find the ultimate, single rule for action. This multiplicity of ways of knowing exists within a socio-cultural framework. You cannot isolate knowledge from the context that produces it.

It was assumed that an art-based research paradigm was an appropriate and valid form of inquiry for this study. Artists and teachers tend to have an antipathy to positivist enterprises that dominate much global monitoring of standards. Bearing this in mind, the book adopts an approach that aims to listen and see in an in-depth fashion. Similarly, while more qualitative research methodologies have been chosen as having greatest applicability to this study, these have not been viewed as the single, correct methodology and so the presentation of findings begins in each section with a summary of key issues (presented as dot points), followed by summaries of the meta-analysis of key statistical information. The statistical data is then explained and exemplified through specific qualitative responses, examples at the national or local level, and stories from teachers, children and artists. It is hoped that this combination of broad-based data and descriptive narrative allows issues to be fore grounded and patterns to emerge.

Like a good artwork, there are no simple predictable patterns. Aligned to both the research and critique agendas, this study is both descriptive and analytical in nature and strives to expound upon the meanings inherent in national policy and classroom practices. Yet to find these at times elusive meanings, themes have been used to organise the analysis. Just as one would not judge a song against the same criteria as one might judge a watercolour painting, the nature of the reporting process should align to the characteristics of what is being studied.

This study was positioned within the education and arts/cultural disciplines so the following chapter – chapter 2 – is recognition of contextual and historical aspects of practice and reflections on the significance of the learning environment. It presents an overview of the social and historical milieu surrounding arts education policy and practices. It contextualises any reading of current practices not only through a general historical reading, but also importantly in terms of issues of future citizenship, global economies and expansion of the creative sectors of society. Within this context, chapter 2 outlines the major challenges facing arts education and the shortcomings of current practices.

As with understanding an artwork, play or piece of music or dance, the book endorses the investigation of both the individual and the universal simultaneously and accommodates the layers of meaning that are difficult to operationalise in more linear research approaches. Chapter 3 outlines the research process that forms the basis of the findings presented in this book. It recognises that arts-rich education reflects highly complex social issues and that no single inquiry model can be developed that can 'answer a given problem'. This chapter challenges the idea that educational research is about asking defined questions and seeking 'an answer' or 'answers' to those questions.

Having situated the book in terms of context and underpinning research, chapter 4 takes a big picture by presenting the findings of research that maps the national and global terrain of arts education. Through an analysis of policy and beliefs, this chapter overviews and exemplifies the scope and nature of arts education. It asks core questions about the nature of arts education and questions existing definitions, and specified inclusions, and importantly, exclusions. Chapter 4 attempts to analysis responsibility chains in terms of implementation of arts education policy and examines what happens beyond policy rhetoric to the place of the arts within core educational entitlements. Importantly, the chapter concludes by making the clear distinction between education *in the arts* and education *through the arts*.

Chapter 5 moves beyond the rhetoric of policy to analyse arts education in practice. Initially, this involves examining the arts learning environment and the delivery chain in terms of ensuring arts-education provisions are met. A key focus of this chapter is on teacher education, especially in the area of professional development for teachers and artists.

The goals and indications of quality in arts-rich education are extrapolated and exemplified in chapter 6. Following on from the ideas presented in chapters 4 and 5, chapter 6 assumes that policy supports the arts, and that the environment and the teachers' expertise in conducive to effective programmes, yet asks the questions 'How do we know what is *good* arts education when it occurs?' The extensive case studies that underpin this book have been analysed in chapter 6 to present a clear –

and to a large extent unequivocal – list of the structures and methods that determine quality arts provisions within education and present a blueprint for the development of arts-rich models for the future.

Chapter 7 focuses on the child and young person and the benefits that accrue through quality arts-rich education. The emphasis in this chapter is on determining the impacts – academically, socially and emotionally – of high quality arts pro-grammes within the lives of young people. It compares the claimed goals with data and examples of actual impacts from very diverse examples of quality practices from around the world.

This research was not just about conversations and critique, but also contained imaginative and pragmatic visions for a range of possible futures. To this end, chapter 8 summarises the major conclusions of the research and outlines a vision for future directions in arts education. Change is a non-linear process that involves people in constructing new and sophisticated information. Simply applying rigid models or reproducing a single conceptual map is not the way to promote change. A reification and recipes approach to knowledge rarely leads to capturing of hearts and minds essential to engender change and innovation. Furthermore, it is impossible to conceive of a pedagogical theory or an implementation strategy that addresses all situations in an area of inquiry as diverse and interesting as arts education. It is acknowledged that in order for pedagogical practices to be successful, they must be adapted to their particular social, historical, cultural and economic contexts. So while chapter 8 provides pragmatic suggestions for improving the quality of arts education as core within general education, it is assumed that any programmes resulting from the analysis and visions articulated in this book need to be designed to meet varying contexts.

Finally, this book operates in a two-way relationship with the reader and hence interpretation remains open to the multiple constructions held by various audiences. It is hoped that this book starts conversations and is catalytic of action. The book is designed to communicate with people at all levels within the policy and implementation chain.

Chapter 2:
Social, political and historical context for thinking about arts education

Introduction

Context is germane to an understanding of arts education. As Emery (1999) contends, the arts exist as constructions of the collective beliefs of society and the principles upon which that context is formulated directly impact on the nature of art. Context is not a single entity. As is the case studies used to inform this book exemplify, the context is a complex social, political and economic milieu in which theory and practice are enacted (Freedman and Hernandez 1998). The context for this study is not a single, static quality that can be described with any sense of universality at the commencement of the book. Rather context closely resembles what Keifer-Boyd (1996: 37) describes as a tangled web of "shifting, contradictory realities (that) coexist, collide and interface".

Zagreb Young IDEA
Workshop 2005
(dialogic sculptures
of rage, Zagreb).
Photo courtesy of
Dan Baron Cohen.

Context can be read at several levels. This book explores context by looking at the histories of arts education, how these are being enacted at the policy level and then case studies of actual practices. Historical context is part of the way meanings are made. Moreover, it should be emphasised that context is considered to be dynamic and even as it is written about; it is inevitably evolving and metamorphosing, and with these changes, interpretation and meaning also change.

Social and historical influence on arts education

There are a number of historical factors that influence the context of arts education and have acted to produce, at least in part, some of the problems facing arts education. It is not the intention within this book to produce a definitive and complete history of art education, but rather highlight general trends that contribute to the nature of arts education. Global interconnection is increasing in complexity and theory and practice are tending to be "appropriated internationally" (Freedman and Hernandez 1998: 183). To this extent, dominant histories of arts education tend to be played out to a greater or lesser extent within the arts education policy and practices of countries around the world. Freedman and Hernandez (1998: 187) argue that:

> "National" curriculum guidelines for art education look remarkably similar across countries, international programs (such as the *International Baccalaureate*) provide leadership in curriculum development and student assessment, and computer networks enable students to easily access people and art from around the world.

The result of this internationalisation is that there appears to be relatively fixed common goals that are generally accepted internationally and impact directly upon local practice. By contrast, Errazuriz (1998) maintains that it is not always advisable or possible to justify local art instruction in terms of these internationally communicated, foreign aims. Errazuriz (1998: 177) bemoans that:

> Too often educational systems are mere copies of those devised in other countries and it is an essential task of educators to redefine and remodel their own educational programs in the light of their countries' aims and their actual social, economic and cultural conditions.

Freedman (1998) suggests that there are a number of more localised influences that impact on art education practices including state regulation, cultural ideals and teacher professionalism.

Art education histories can be examined from a number of different viewpoints. Hernandez (1998) proposes at least six possible frames that can be used as a focus for historical contextualisation including: content, values, socio-economic relations, debates, influences and names and books. Freedman and Hernandez (1998: 58) also suggest broadening any reflective historical study to include "social, political, artistic and educational events that create bodies of knowledge and a structural network which provides a level of understanding of influences beyond the content of the field."

Similarly, past and present histories combine and overlap forming both macro and micro histories that impact on the actions of an individual arts teacher or a particular arts programme. Histories also serve to underpin imaginings of possible futures in arts education. Foucault (1998) makes a case that individuals exist within a system of conventions, rules, norms and discourses which in effect 'speak' that person, making them converse and think in certain ways. Assuming Foucault's view, histories are about tracing the ideas and how these are evident in arts education processes. Carroll (1997: 190) stresses the importance of histories in the study of art education when she cautions:

> If the art education community is ambivalent towards its history and the beliefs and values and practices embedded in it, then the field is destined to repeat mistakes, weaken its successes by instructional stagnation, and expend its energies and resources on irrelevant curricular questions and instructional efforts.

The results of this world study suggest that a community – and education – pays a clear price for "blind" practices.

Several major trends in art education impact on arts education practices as they are experienced around the world. There could be considerable contention about the way these complex educational and arts ideas have been simplified into seemingly discreet influences, but the intention of this book is not to provide a comprehensive history of arts education – though perhaps such a publication would be timely. In this case, the justification for providing the groupings that follow is to summarise the main philosophical, ideological and at times pragmatic considerations which interplay to give the kinds of arts education we see in most countries around the world. They also serve to underpin the milieu evident in policy and in some way account for the eclectic and diverse policies witnessed at a national, state or local level. These influences include ideas that I have grouped as follows:

- **Technocratic art** presents the view that the arts are comprised of a series of skills that serve the needs of industry and a desire for a capable skilled workforce;

- **Child art** views the arts as a natural development phenomenon of children, governed by the child's physical and psychological growth and the need to freely communicate their needs and emotions;
- **Arts as expression** occurs through free engagement in arts experiences that stress creativity, imagination and authenticity of outcomes, implying a level of therapeutic benefit to the individual;
- **Arts as cognition** focuses on the arts as a form of intellectual inquiry capable of being studied from a critical framework and that the arts embody unique forms of thinking in the process of creating artworks;
- **Arts as aesthetic response** explores sensory and perceptual definitions of art through disciplined inquiry into the principles underpinning the aesthetic;
- **Arts as symbolic communication** treats the arts as a language form whereby people communicate;
- **Arts as a cultural agent** accentuates the role of the arts in social action, social reconstruction and the role of culture in society, and;
- **Postmodernism** challenges traditional definitions of arts and questions the physicality and performativity of the arts and the definability of a concept called 'the arts'.

The *technocratic paradigm* for art education emerged in the late 1800s and subsequently gained popularity through the South Kensington approach, most evident in the visual arts in terms of industrial drawing and design education. Chalmers (1998) contends that this view valued manual dexterity and coordination and was largely taught through disciplined, reproductive exercises. During this time, the arts became identified with the productive domain and skills were paramount to knowledge or conceptual development (Benjamin 1996).

By contrast, *the child art movement* resulted from the merging of child development theorists and the psychological study of the arts. It considered that children's artistic and creative activities could be used to develop the child's intelligence and democratic personality. Drawings, play and drama were seen as images of the young mind, mirroring the soul and allowing scientific investigation of the child's thoughts, feelings and development. Franz Cizek (1921) argued that the arts (in particular visual arts) were a natural aspect of human development, the absence of which impaired mental growth and social fitness. He felt that arts education developed children's capacities to give expression to their feelings and ideas. Cizek believed that every child had a natural tendency towards creative and artistic expression. He argued that this natural tendency needed to be fostered through creative and imaginative activities. He favoured giving children unbridled freedom to express their ideas. Under this approach, teachers adopted roles as facilitators, providing a stimulating environment, adequate and varied art materials, and praise for the children's efforts but did not direct or influence children's creative processes. Marion Richardson (1948) continued the work of Cizek, recommending an approach to arts education based on stimulating the children's imagination with "unconventional teaching", "evoking mental images" through questioning and conversation (Thistlewood 1998: 140). Cizek and Richardson's work was fuelled by child psychologists and child development theorists such as Viktor Lowenfeld (1964), John Dewey (1934) and Jean Piaget (1954) who theorised that children progressed through delineated and naturally occurring creative stages. Arts education became centred on ensuring the children achieved certain developmental stages and focussed on different levels of growth of the child. Lovgren and Karlsson (1998: 96) argued that the role of the teacher in this approach became supervisory so as not to interfere with the creative process described as the "organic growth of the child". Teachers became less clear about their role in arts education and arts education policy loosely referred to concepts such as creativity, feeling and expression without clarifying the scope and applicability of these ideas within the context of education.

Allied to the child art movement was the *arts as expression* movement. While sharing many aspects of the child arts movement in relation to freedom and the importance of the art making process, the arts as expression rationale was based strongly on the belief that the arts were vital to the emotional wellbeing of the child. This view stressed that children's enjoyment was paramount. The arts were seen as being a place of freedom and recreation that ensured a balanced curriculum, catering for both the intellectual and emotional needs of the child. It was regarded as a leisure activity that was good for the soul and counteracted the regimental nature of more academic pursuits. The arts furthering the cause of democracy through freedom of expression and spontaneity. The notion of the arts being primarily a mode of expression tended to have three main manifestations within education policy and practice. That is, art as expression of the individual through the release of the subconscious; art as the romantic notation of 'free arts' that gains ascendancy over culture; and expressive arts as a therapeutic device to enable children to cope with increasingly complex social order. While each of these manifestations is connected to the belief that arts are the expression of the inner soul, the purpose behind the release of expression through art was different.

In the 1980's arts education began to shift to a more discipline, intellectual and cognitive base. Arts educators formed into strong professional bodies – especially in visual arts, music and drama – which were keen to promote their specific art disciplines. In a reaction to the perceived marginalisation of the arts as an expressive, recreational activity, art teachers – through their discipline based professional associations – asserted the intellectual rigour, cognitive benefits and academic rationales for various components in arts education. Much research was commissioned arguing the value of music, visual arts, drama and dance. Concurrently with this, economic rationalist thinking has questioning the cost effectiveness and value of the arts within education, most famously in California during the early 1980s (Schrag 1999).

Child-survivors of the 1996 massacre of nineteen Landless Movement peasants contributing to the transformation of burnt brazil-nut trees into a community sculpture and national monument of healing and justice (10m x 15m x 25m, Eldorado dos Carajas, Para, Brazil 1999). Photo courtesy of Dan Baron Cohen.

There was a shift away from behavioural and emotional rationales for the arts to more *cognitive approaches*. Each discipline within arts education argued that their particular art form provided unique ways in which mental and intellectual development was communicated through symbolic expression. The child was viewed as a "conscious critical individual" (Lovgren and Sten-Gosta 1998) and child art and creative art movements gave way to notions of art as knowledge and an academic skill. Allied to this, the emphasis on individualisation became subsumed in the need to build knowledge of historical exemplars of best art practice (Greer 1992). The cognitive approach to art moved away from child models to reliance upon studying acclaimed art works as examples of best practice in the discipline. The academicism of the arts meant that children were expected to function as cognisant artists. The process was still important, but it had become the design or problem solving process rather than the 'creative' process. Children were expected to observe, plan, create, develop skills, reflect upon and evaluate their artworks or performance. The teachers' role became to scaffold this process, through the provision of the skills necessary for the children to engage in the problem solving process and through arts appreciation to expose the children to examples of quality art that could be used as the basis of critiquing their own work.

At the commencement of the 20th century, arts education in many Western countries was closely aligned to a European view of *aesthetics*. Aesthetics was associated with being civilised and cultured. Based on the French and Italian notion that art was a cultural achievement and a visible sign of education and social class, it was felt that study of the fine arts and classics was a discipline of the mind. Children would study classical styles and the arts became the epitome of beauty, class and culture. Studying the aesthetic dimension was seen to enhance the mind and acculturate children (Eagleton 1990). Under the aesthetic agenda, arts education looked to arts community to find models of practice, and academic disciplines such as arts critics, historians and sociology informed arts education ideals. Much later in the 20th century, but allied to the aesthetic trend, artists-in-residence programmes were introduced into schools as a way to foster community interest in aesthetic inquiry and to provide professional models for the children. Transdisciplinary and interdisciplinary studies were also introduced into the school curriculum in the belief that education could occur through the arts and aesthetic structures could be applied to other areas of the curriculum.

The introduction of television and the increased push to global communication focused attention on the *communicative* and *symbolic* aspects of art. Symbols can be used to effectively communicate information, knowledge and beliefs. The arts communicate through non-discursive means using a visual, musical and dramatic vocabulary that is expressive, cultural and symbolic. Herbert Read (1970) saw the potential of visual communication as a medium for effective international exchange. He considered the arts as providing, "A language of symbols that communicate meaning without hindrance from country to country across the centuries" (Read 1970: 233). Herbert Read could not have foreseen the impact of computer technology and the World Wide Web and the manner in which it foregrounds visual and aesthetic communication codes. In recent times there has been a growing interest in what is termed visual or multimodal "literacy". The use of the literacy metaphor is recognition of the complexity of "reading" the visual and aesthetic codes widely used in contemporary communication. The classical writers, especially Aristotle (1965), emphasised the artistic element in daily activities, speaking about 'the art of rhetoric', 'the art of politics' etc. This usage of the term 'art' is being revisited in relation to the aestheticisation of modes of communication prevalent in the new media. It is about the "art" of reading, the "art of speaking" and the "art" of gaining meaning from images, sounds, movements and dramatic action. In response to this multimodal trend in communication, arts education has had to work in an interdisciplinary way with other curriculum areas to help children read and understand the aesthetic symbols that are used to communicate the complexities of life. Under this conception, the arts operate to convey information and as a powerful language for arousing social and cultural consciousness. Education is thus very much like 'political activities' in the writings of philosopher Hannah Arendt: "the Greeks always used such metaphors as flute playing, dancing, healing, and seafaring to distinguish political from other activities, that is they drew their analogies from those arts in which virtuosity of performance is decisive" (Arendt 1983: 153). Quality education is an area where virtuosity of performance is necessary.

Allied to the symbolic and communicative potential of the arts, there has been an increased focus on the notion of the *arts as a cultural agent*. In this model, the role of the teacher is as a mediator of culture, bringing to children socially derived perspectives of cultural refinement and discernment. Curricula founded on this view propose that an awareness of cultural heritage is an essential aspect of understanding human experience and establishing a cultural identity. With a belief that arts education assists the development of cultural awareness there is recognition of art as a force for civilising humanity. The cultural aim of arts education reflects the significance of the arts as a legacy of historical civilisation and national heritage. In this way, the arts become a political force. Freedman (1998: 187) notes, "Art education has been influenced by political initiatives, social priorities and cultural crises." Allied to this approach, is the view that democratisation of culture can be achieved through arts education. Under a democratic arts curriculum all children receive cultural education, especially in relation to developing an appreciation of the arts, in the belief that such inclusions assist in ensuring social equity. This approach views the arts as being a proactive social agent. This reflects the influence of social sciences and politics within the arts community and the view that the arts can display and challenge social ideals and exemplify social constructions of the self as artist or performer within a cultural context. This idea may originate from Dewey's (1934) view of the arts as the expression of the relationship between material, process and ideal. The artwork or performance exists as the embodied realisation of the interaction between people and their environment. Dewey extended the idea of self-expression to include notions of social intent in the artist's work.

The arts have emerged in the post second world war baby boomers as an expression for *youth and alternative culture*. Young people saw visual, musical and dramatic symbolism as a way of forging an identity. Youth culture challenged the models of a dominant culture and instead began forming a cultural unity through the arts. The expressive powers of the arts allows counter groups to push agendas of cultural change. The aesthetic values of adults were questioned and the growing leisure industry, fuelled by an affluent youth market led to an explosion in visual and musical culture apparent in everything from sports shoes to hair colour!

It could be argued that this aesthetic explosion led to ideas of *postmodernism* within the arts. Postmodernism implies the centrality of culture in any interpretation of the arts by considering critical and cultural analysis as being more significant than formal analysis. Adopting a democratic social code of discourse, there is a breaking down of barriers between art, everyday experiences, the fine arts and popular culture. Analysis focuses on relationships and interrelationships, issues of social and personal transformations, and semiotics and deconstruction. Skills and technology are less important and intentions and meanings are more important. Diamond and Mullen (1999: 22) note: "Postmodernists replace the idea of a single radiating self as a stable, unified, conscious subject with that of a light-headed, fluid, constantly changing community of multiple selves with struggles within and for consciousness".

Artistic and creative expression therefore exists as a construction of inner thoughts. Postmodernism is about sensed arts experience that are personal, individual, emotional and provocative. Foster (1983: x) contends that postmodernist art practice, "is not defined in relation to a given medium ... but rather in relation to the logical operations on a set of cultural terms." Postmodernism rejects notions of universal or privileged interpretation, preferring interpretations based on personal experiences and acceptance of the coexistence of multiple positions and competing narratives.

It can also be argued that postmodernism is not so much a theory about the arts but rather the way life is now. Life is about computerisation, internationalisation, televisuals, mass media, mass marketing and hyper-reality. The world has itself become more real than real and hyper reality undermines some of the fundamental theories that have informed art practice. For example, cultural awareness is often used as a rationale for art education, yet what is culture in the World Wide Web? Similarly "beauty" is often seen as a pivotal point in defining aesthetics, yet in a world of enhanced images, falsification and digitalisation, architects of beauty are able to modify personal perceptions of image and beauty.

Challenges in arts education

A number of research studies conducted over the past 10 years at the national or regional level have indicated that arts education frequently drop below acceptable levels of provision within general education. Holt's study (1997: 94-95) in the United Kingdom found that arts education fell below what could be considered 'satisfactory' performance in over one third of schools studied. This study concluded that there was considerable concern over the quality of arts education learning within England, particularly in relation to the training of teachers and the types of activities being completed by children. Similarly, Chia (1995: 6) describes Singaporean arts education as being characterised by:

Apathetic teachers ... who rely on their old 'stand-by' favourites which have little educational purpose ... there is a sense of aimlessness about art teaching in many primary schools ... there is a need for proper training of teachers who will teach art.

Eisner (1997: 62) writes of the poor standard of arts education in American elementary schools, summarised by the comment:

I have emphasised some of the salient characteristics of the teaching of art at the elementary level because I believe that is where art programs are weakest and because that is where I believe they are particularly important in the child's educational development.

Australian studies on arts education (Ashton 1999) present a similar picture. The arts are often perceived to have the potential for disruptive class behaviour, and hence many teachers seek activities that allow tight control of children's behaviour and use limited resources that are 'easy to clean-up'. As Ashton (1998: 8) notes, "I lament how in our primary schools, art often serves as a window dresser, is conspicuously spasmodic, and how its curriculum status is akin to a twilight zone with systematic documents few and far between."

Wilson (1999: 6) identified the major problems in arts education as being:
- The belief that arts activities are developmental (for example, creative development and manipulative development) rather than for learning specific things about the arts;
- The belief that child artistic and creative development is precious and that it can best unfold where adult influence is kept to a minimum;
- The belief that young children's attitudes, beliefs, values and knowledge with regard to arts can be changed in a relatively short period of time in the classroom, often taught by generalists who themselves have little knowledge of art.

Wilson (1997) argues that what happens in school in relation to arts and cultural education is closer to *bricolage*, more reflective of superficial busy work than sustained arts development (Levi-Strauss 1966). Holt (1997) noted a clear lack of purpose and direction in arts education. Parmenter (1995: 8) commented that the arts are frequently viewed as a fun subject between the more rigorous disciplines. Arts-based education is too often characterised by a lack of coherent or sequential programmes and activities that tend to trivialise arts learning. As Taylor (1986: 258) writes: "Teachers provided materials, gave the class a title and left them to 'get on with it' [This] indicates the need for a concerted in-service programme but particularly points to the scale of the teacher-training problem."

Cunliffe (1990: 278) notes that teachers, "frequently repeat with their pupils many of the art activities they did themselves as students." The result of lack of specific content and sequence in arts education is at best a collection of activities with little coherent purpose, or at worst no art education provided to children at all.

Poor quality arts education may be particularly evident within 'at risk' school communities, where there is a perception that literacy and vocational education take precedence over the arts. Extensive arts-rich programmes tend to be most prevalent in affluent and high achieving schools. Furthermore, while the benefits of the arts within education have been recorded in a number of international studies, further research needs to critically examine the most effective ways of developing quality arts interventions within the school. There is growing interest in the potential of arts-rich programmes in education. This is particularly so for children who may be marginalized from the education system and are – to use a contested term – *at risk* of not fulfilling their artistic or educational potential.

Young people deemed to be "at risk" are those with a constellation of inter-related risk factors, either within themselves, or within the community in which they live. Factors that identify an "at risk" community include things such as substance abuse, poor educational and employment histories, poor health, welfare intervention and dysfunctional family backgrounds (Cunneen and White 1995; Jones 1998). In recent years, there has been increasing interest in the potential of arts-rich educational programmes to enhance the learning outcomes of more marginalized student groups. However, there has been a lack of rigorous international evidence that examines either the process or the outcomes of the use of such programmes. This issue is further compounded by the difficulty of developing a research methodology that allows for the gathering of what could be considered "hard evidence" of impact and implementation strategies.

It was within a background of these issues that it was decided to undertake research aimed at gathering research demonstrating the impact (if any) of arts-rich programmes on the education of children and young people around the world. Particular emphasis was given to students who may be marginalised or 'at risk' in terms of fulfilling their educational and artistic potential.

It was within the general historical and social context – and informed by earlier research that bemoaned the quality of arts provisions within general education – that the research underpinning this book was commenced. It was felt strongly at the outset of the research that the arts may offer some positive impact for education in general, and specifically for those children for whom education has failed to be engaging, challenging or meaningful. It was also assumed that a global inquiry into arts-rich education may shed light on the nature of quality provisions and the impact of these on the educational potential of children.

Chapter 3:
Underpinning research

The data

This book is based on the results of a written survey that was sent to 151 key people involved in arts education provisions within 75 countries. The survey was designed by the research team[4] in collaboration with both questionnaire designers and an advisory panel.[5] This group evaluated the survey for both clarity and relevance to a range of countries and cultural contexts. The survey was primarily available in English, but on request, was also available in Spanish and French. The survey was distributed in electronic form through the network of Arts, Culture and Education Ministries through the IFACCA data base and through UNESCO arts and education national representatives. While respondents were encouraged to complete the form electronically, hard copies were also provided where this was not possible. In a limited number of cases, surveys were also distributed to individuals or organisations whose reputation and status meant that they were able to complete the survey and provide national insight (see Appendix 2 for a list of responding organisations).

Despite this extensive process of global distribution, one flaw within this process was that the surveys did not always reach the people 'on the ground' who may have been most likely to provide a detailed picture of arts education in practice. This is problematic of education policy in general, where the policy makers (to whom the survey was primarily sent) may not have the *bottom-up* knowledge required to most accurately present a picture of arts education practices at the *coalface*. However, in many countries, the surveys were passed onto teachers, arts workers and people conducting research projects within the country to complete.

The survey was distributed between October and December 2004. Responses were accepted up until the end of January 2005. A total of 37 responses were received from countries and arts, culture and educational organisations representing groups of countries (a copy of the survey is contained in Appendix 1). While the N is not overwhelming in itself, the fact that the responding countries represent a broad mix of countries from all parts of the world means that the findings are likely to be representative of the UNESCO member countries.[6] Further, as each of these 37

---

4   The author in consultation with Tereza Wagner, Christopher Madden, and Matt Qvortrup.
5   Gillian Gardiner, Sarah Gardner, Michael Anderson, Arnold Aprill, Maureen O'Rourke, Rod Parnall, Robin Pascoe, Barbara Piscitelli, Simon Spain, und Tereza Wagner.
6   Responses were not received from the Middle East. Following subsequent rounds of invitations a submission was received from a respondent based in Jordan. Whether this low level of responses is indicative of an under prioritisation of arts education in these countries is impossible to determine on the basis of the information received as part of this study.

countries each submitted three research studies the number of respondents is actually higher than the figure may initially suggest. In fact, some of these studies were omnibus studies in their own right, e.g. one of Canada's submitted research studies was a national study of arts education. Similar submissions were received from Australia and the European Council. Moreover, additional case-studies were received from 6 countries, which had not initially returned the survey. While these could not be included in the quantitative part of the study there were incorporated in the qualitative analysis. (Appendices 2, 3 and 4 detail the responses from countries)

In addition to the quantitative and qualitative parts of the survey, countries were also invited to submit up to three case studies and visual records. Each country was asked to select research-based case studies that examined the impact of the arts within education. In terms of these case studies, we accepted the data as it was presented and did not individually scrutinise these to determine their veracity. It can be said, however, that as each country was asked to select the best research studies that there was an embedded level of at least reputational quality control. It was also important to the research team to avoid the temptation to apply a universal model of 'good' research or standards of arts-rich education, but rather to seek broader derivatives of how this may be enacted at the national or local level.

Once all the surveys were received, further efforts were made to seek responses from geographic regions under-represented in the data sets. These attempts were only partially successful due to the difficulty of locating key arts education contacts within these countries.

Carrying out this research presented methodological challenges. On the one hand, it was necessary to use a relatively tight definition of the arts in order to gather comparable overall information about the extent, content, and impact of the different programmes. On the other hand these definitions were often too narrow to capture the full extend of the programmes. Arts education – as defined in the quantitative part of the project – aim:

- To pass on cultural heritage to young people, and;
- To enable them to create their own artistic language and to contribute to their global development (emotional and cognitive).

Quantitative findings were verified through cross checking with over 60 qualitative case studies. Respondents of the survey were given opportunities for citing examples of pertinent case studies and, in general, invited to give examples of programmes that fall outside the definition of arts employed in this study. In order to assess the impact of arts-rich programmes, the qualitative and quantitative information gathered from the extensive survey conducted between October 2004 and January 2005, was analysed. The following questions guided the analysis:

- How was the teaching or arts-rich programmes organised?
- Who are responsible for curriculum development and implementation of arts-rich programmes?

- What are the differences between the arts-rich programmes taught in the different countries?
- What determines the differences in content from country to country?
- What can be expected or recommended of arts-rich programmes in the future?

The analysis

The analysis involved quantitative interpretation and the scrutiny of statistical data through direct reference to qualitative comments and written questionnaire responses. This analysis was cross-referenced to information contained within the written and visual case studies supplied. The case studies have principally been presented as they were received. While the information contained within them provided further sources for verification of the survey data, no attempt was made to analyse the veracity of the case studies or to draw comparisons. Where responses were received in languages other than English, these were translated prior to analysis. As far as possible, exact quotations from the qualitative data have been used to support the interpretations and analysis made in this book. It was considered that the researchers, teachers and artists that provided the case studies were best placed to derive meaning from the context in which each of the case studies were sited. For this reason, all qualitative comments appear as close as possible to the way they were reported.

Journeys into the imagination. This image shows a child's journey adopting the role of an early gold miner immigrant (Education and Arts Partnership Initiative, Australia). Photograph courtesy of the author.

The bringing together of often quite disparate pieces of evidence and research that strongly represented localised context posed some analytical challenges. For example, some countries reported major policy positions and key curriculum initiatives, while other countries chose to exemplify a country's policy and practices through a series of very localised case studies. Similarly, many countries acknowledged that there was a deviation from the overall national or regional position and the actual 'coalface' reality. In these instances it was often the case that respondents may report the 'official' position in the quantitative sections of the survey, while present a quite different and at times contradictory position in the qualitative comments.

To provide a coherent framework for analysis, a thematic approach has been used to present the findings of the research. This approach aimed to bring key ideas or elements of policy and practice into meaningful conjunction and to include both quantitative and qualitative findings to explicate the issue being analysed. Furthermore, contradictions and internal inconsistencies were included to show the complexities evident around many of the issues discussed.

Problems concerning quantitative interpretation

It was the intention at the outset of this research to conduct a quantitative survey of the content, nature, and impact of arts education. It became soon apparent, however, that such an approach was both methodologically problematic and practically demanding. Quantitative approaches are based on the premise that complex phenomena can be reduced to simple entities that can be subjected to numerical analysis. Already at the stage of the construction of the survey, it became clear that even the most elementary question defied the reductionist approach.

For example, a seemingly simple question like 'How many hours a week do you spend on arts education?' contains within it a host of essentially contested concepts. As the concepts can be interpreted differently, the result is likely to be that the answers will reflect different perceptions. Yet, these differences are hidden in the seeming uniformity of the answers. For example: Is there a discrepancy between mandated policy requirement regarding number of hours or hours taught; does merely hours taught equate with quality provisions? Or, when calculating hours of instruction do we include only hours of instruction particularly within the arts, or also subjects which make use of artistic pedagogies? In addition to these already difficult questions the complexities of the definitions of the arts within different educational contexts render the question statistically meaningless.

Moreover, while statistics are useful for comparing cases, there is always a danger that we overlook the special cases by compounding them all into arithmetic figures.

This problem is increasingly acknowledged in the social sciences: "The laws of statistics are valid only where large numbers or long periods are involved, and acts and events can statistically appear only as deviations and fluctuations. The justification of statistics is that deeds and events are rare occurrences in everyday life and history" (Arendt 1958: 42). Acknowledging this it was deemed more useful to adopt a qualitative approach which takes diversity of interpretation as its point of departure.

However, there is clearly room for quantitative approaches. In spite of the inherent limitations of the quantitative paradigm, it is deemed an imperative to have at least some numerical baselines against which policies can be evaluated. Neither of these approaches can be regarded as panaceas. The research team believe that a pragmatic approach is warranted and justified – even though we acknowledge the methodological problems which this raises. In line with current practice within sociology the study has thus adopted a modified triangulation approach, i.e. a methodology which contains a pragmatic mix of qualitative, narratological and quantitative approaches. We contend that the value of the arts is most likely to be revealed through approaches that accord most closely to the creative nature of artistic expression. As Lisa Jane Disch (1996: 106) eloquently writes: "A well-crafted story shares with the most elegant theories the ability to bring to light a version of the World that transforms the way people see that it seems never to have been otherwise."

This global study is not alone in having encountered the difficulty of measuring the impact of arts-rich education. Many of the case studies contained within this report acknowledged the limitations of such approaches. Even where these are large scale national research projects the methodological challenges are commonly recognised. For example, in Scotland an extensive research project reported in this survey aimed to provide robust evidence of the social and economic impact of arts, culture and sport within education. This project devised methodologies to examine the benefits of participation in the arts, cultural and sporting activities and the under-representation of certain groups. This research involved extensive surveys to determine an evidence base for the impact of the arts and found that there were impacts within social, economic, health and educational benefits. However, the researchers recognised that gaps in the available evidence, especially in relation to data collection methods, and longitudinal studies existed. In particular they conceded that more research was needed within under-represented groups and in relation to the role of creativity in education and problem solving, cognitive and social development.

The decision to adopt a triangulated approach has a number of implications. One in particular needs to be singled out, namely the reporting of the statistical findings. We appreciate that questions can have more answers than one; that the responses to

45

the survey are not mutually exclusive. When presenting the quantitative data we have *not* cumulated the findings, but presented figures for each section in the form of tables that do not necessarily add up to a 100.

In choosing this approach it is acknowledged that the complexities of quantitative data across countries and within a field as diverse as the arts predicates approaches that are transparent and comprehensive rather than reductionist.

With these considerations in mind the survey and case studies were analysed to reveal the following key issues in art education:
- Definitions;
- Inclusions;
- Funding sources and partnerships;
- Responsibility for the design of policy and delivery;
- Extent of inclusion in national education policy and curricula;
- The perceived role of arts in education;
- Implementation and deliver;
- Teacher education and continuing professional education;
- Goals;
- Quality;
- Impact on learning in the arts;
- Impact on academic achievement;
- Improvements in student attitudes;
- The value of creative partnerships in building teacher professionalism;
- Community building;
- Creativity and imagination;
- Health and well-being of children and youth;
- Main challenges;
- Research methodologies, and;
- ICT literacies and technical skills.

These main issues were derived from the data and used as a framework for analysis, interpretation and reporting.

Chapter 4:
The scope and nature of arts education

Introduction

This chapter uses the data from the survey to map the territory of arts education. It presents both a global picture of arts education and highlights significant variations to this overall representation which give local arts education programmes their characteristics.[7]

This book re-examines what is considered as knowledge in arts education and what constitutes quality artistic and cultural learning within education. It is acknowledged that arts education is what Wilson (1997: 2) terms as "socially constructed", reflecting "conflicting sets of values that abound in pluralistic societies, in the worlds of art, and the worlds of education". There is a view that the arts lack focus. Numerous and at times conflicting aims – and supposed outcomes – are attributed to arts education with limited research to substantiate these claims. To be able to understand arts education practices, there is a need to ascertain the goals and intentions governing these practices.

The arts have been included in some form or another in education for many years, yet the problem of quality and the differences between espoused policy and classroom practices have been documented in almost all countries. The Council of Europe in its report *Culture, Creativity and the Young Project* noted that:

> The study of arts education provision in these countries in many cases also shows an inconsistency between national policy statements, which strongly emphasises the importance of the cultural dimension of education and of encouraging artistic and aesthetic development in young people, and the existing practice, where the status of and provision for arts education appear less prominent. Moreover, emphasis on academic and technical education often places the arts in the periphery of the curricula encouraging polarities between the arts and the sciences. Such facts are reinforced by the existence, in many countries, of separate ministries of education and culture often resulting in the development of independent responsibilities.

It could be argued that the arts, more than any other area of education, has been subject to waves of passing educational practices, that rather than building strong programmes, have detrimentally resulted in scattered approaches with little educa-

---

7   Each section reports a key theme. The dot points at the beginning of each section are the main findings and key implications of that section.

tional merit. The child development approach to arts education (Lowenfeld and Brittain 1964) favoured a non-interventionist approach, whereby the teacher adopted the role of monitor of children's arts development rather than active teaching of art. This view (Cizek 1921) allowed the 'non-teaching' of the arts to be legitimised as a method of protecting the sacrosanct, naïve and expressive quality of children's creative and artistic actions. The arts continue to be characterised in many schools as being a series of experiments or experiences with little cogent direction or planning. The children rarely have an opportunity to develop the skills and understandings needed to work well in any one or more disciplines that build an arts-rich programme. Such ad hoc approaches reinforce in children the belief that they are not 'good at the arts' as they are constantly trying new things but never developing any sense of competency. It is within this context of the range of socio-political conditions, economic restraints and conflicting values that this study is conceived.

What does art education include?

- Definitions of arts education are varied and context specific
- Music, drawing, painting and craft appear in almost all countries as part of arts education
- Universal notions of arts education may not be sufficient for describing the full cultural impact of the arts within certain cultures

The definitions of arts education are varied and context specific and while the *arts* are often talked about in a generic or universal way, inclusions within arts education vary significantly according to the economic development of a country.

At the outset, it is clear that the term 'arts education' is used in diverse ways across cultures. While this makes comparison of data more difficult, it acknowledges the depth of human engagement in creative arts-related learning and the dynamic nature of arts practices. The data indicates that there is general agreement about some aspects of what should be included under arts education. In over 90% of countries surveyed, music and drawing were part of arts education. Painting and craft were also widely accepted as part of the arts curriculum (80% and 88% respectively). Dance, drama and sculpture, were included in arts education in over 70% of countries (see Table 1).

Areas of arts practice that could be described as new or emerging media, including film, photography, media studies, digital art and design were present in more than 50% of countries but these forms tended to be heavily concentrated within the more economically developed countries. In a number of countries the arts were very culture specific and embedded in the history and heritage of a country. For example, in Afghanistan the *ironpoint* pen (a traditional writing tool) was an important part of the arts curriculum. Similarly, in Fiji the area of weaving is a core part of the curriculum, with several sub-strands including *pandanus*, baskets, mats and tourist souvenirs.

Table 1:   Subjects included in Arts Education (Percentages)[8]

Drawing	96
Music	96
Craft	88
Painting	80
Sculpture	76
Dance	76
Drama	72
Digital art	64
Design	64
Performance	60
Film & Media	52
Others[9]	0
Not available	0

The respondents were permitted to indicate multiple responses
hence the percentages are not cumulative.

There appears to be a hierarchy of arts that has emerged – albeit by default – the visual arts (especially painting and drawing) and music are at the top of the priorities and drama behind this with all other art forms, including multimedia and dance coming in some position after music and fine arts. In many systems, the arts have been almost solely defined as fine arts and music with other areas not being formally considered within the curriculum. As mentioned previously, this compounds the difficulty of tracking provisions of arts-rich education across countries. In some instances, this even differs from state to state or from local area to local area within a national system.

It is the contention of this research to suggest that an adequate provision of arts eduction should include a wide range of arts experiences and include at least art (fine arts, craft and design), drama, music, dance and a range of culturally specific

---

8   The figures in all tables are shown in descending order, not in the order that the questions were asked in the survey.
9   While 'Others' was not reflected in the survey responses, a large number of 'Others' were listed in the comments and qualitative part of the survey. If these had been added to the stastical data, it could have reasonably been suggested that 'Others' would have been the largest grouping.

Education and Arts Partnership Initiative (EAPI) engaging children in the arts as core to quality education. Photo courtesy of the author.

art forms. It is also recommended that at some place within the curriculum children should receive substantial opportunities to participate in making and appreciating literature (including poetry) and new media (including photography, film, digital and others). In addition, it is important to define the contents of arts education by referring to local practices, and contemporary and previous heritage In this regard, practices such as meditation, festival, chanting, and many more should be included as a core part of arts-rich education.

There are also some national systems where the arts are spread across many discipline or curriculum boundaries and where the arts might also be a grouping for the inclusion of quite diverse learning experiences that may be less closely connected to areas that would be generally associated with the arts. For example, within Fiji, health, games and sport also fall under the arts remit.

In other countries, definitions of arts education, and the subsequent content of the curriculum is formed by dividing traditional and modern art forms. For example, within Bhutan a parallel curriculum in the arts exist with both modern and traditional arts being taught. Under the traditional arts curriculum religious art features with children learning the time honoured traditions derived from Buddhism and *Tantric* mythology. The traditional arts curriculum includes 13 specific art forms including *Shing zo, Do zo, par zo, Lha zo, Lug zo, Jim zo, Shap zo, gar zo, Troe zo, Tsha zo, de zo, Tshem zo and Thad zo.* These art forms while generally under what would be considered fine arts and craft grouping include diverse media such as silver and gold, bamboo, stone, wood and cane among many others. In addition, the traditional arts curriculum can include diverse skills such as *butter work* and ceremonial learning including *ritual cake making* and *mandala making*. By contrast, the contemporary or modern art curriculum is centred on very contemporary views of creative industry and includes a wide variety of creative leaning including marketing, advertising, publishing, interactive communication, new media literacies and design. The Ministry supplies very detailed teaching books to cover this diverse area. A key part of this curriculum is also the internationalisation of Bhutanese arts practice through the participation in a number of international exhibitions and competitions.

It could be argued though, that despite the very extensive curriculum in Bhutan, it does not cover drama, dance or music. Conversely, in Cambodia, a similar focus on both traditional and modern arts practices has led to a curriculum that is strongly focused on music, performance, poem and dancing. All children learn traditional Khmer instruments and/or songs and a modern – western – instrument or song. Allied to this, the curriculum also encourages the children to engage in free exploration and creative composition and performance across both traditional and contemporary forms.

Within economically developing countries, definitions of art are broad and indicate cultural awareness and grounding in tradition and way of life. For example, in Barbados, *landship*, *stilt-walking* and *tuk bands* are part of the art education programme, while in Senegal, floral art, numeric art, batik, ceramics, storytelling, fashion, hairstyling, accessorizing and seam-stressing are all included within art education programmes. The Namibian term *Ngoma* sees the arts as being a united whole. While this same term can mean any one of the art forms (eg dance, music, visual arts and drama) it also stands for the communication between the arts and the spirit. Ngoma can also mean 'drum', but under this notion it implies the rhythm or beat of a drum that charges life with energy. It implies a transformation, where the individual becomes transformed by the arts. It encompasses the individual becoming part of the community, linking the past with the future, the heaven with earth, ancestors to children, and the mind to the spirit. The term Ngoma also implies that the action of the arts has a purpose or function larger than the art form itself. It prepares the individual and community for the task, be those tasks the mundane or the profound, the eductive and the spiritually enlightening. Ngoma also sees the arts as integral to society.

Several countries specifically mentioned that cultural heritage study was part of the arts curriculum. This was particularly the case in European countries and seemed to be more apparent in relatively new nation states established in the last 100-150 years. This finding is consistent with nationalist scholars who have established that the process of national building in new countries (Gellner, 1981) is often correlated with a conscious effort to establish 'high culture'. This was also apparent in Asia where countries such as Malaysia and Korea see a strong arts provision as being a key aspect of nation building. In Malaysia, the *Vision 2020* project seeks to build a future Islamic nation through the arts as a way to "develop individuals who are intellectually, spiritually, emotionally and physically balanced and harmonious". To ensure this occurs, this aim of nation building is backed by compulsory centralised arts policy and national curriculum review processes.

The presence – or absence – of literature and literacy study within the arts curriculum seemed to be diverse. Several respondents commented that creative writing and literature were considered part of the arts within national policy but not necessarily taught under the specific auspices of arts education.

Only one country made specific mention of the role of galleries and the critical study of art as being part of the curriculum, but it could be assumed that this idea may have been considered to be embedded in more overarching descriptions of painting, drawing, and music and so on. Similarly, 'aesthetics' was only mentioned as a specific subject within the Slovak Republic, but it could be presupposed as existing within other dimensions of the arts curricula.

Who is responsible for supporting arts education?

- Central government plays a major role in supporting arts education but industry, charities and foundations and individuals are also highly significant
- Galleries, broadcasters and trade unions are also partner organisations in funding and promoting arts education
- The substantial role played by individuals and organisations beyond education is inadequately considered in education policy planning and implementation

Arts education funding comes from a number of sources and partnerships of many different types shore up arts education. The results of the survey indicate the crucial importance of a diversity of supporting agencies in arts education. These agencies need to be considered in policy implementation as it is likely that failure to fully acknowledge the crucial roles played by these within planning models has resulted in the generally poor level of implementation of stated arts policy.

The quantitative and qualitative data suggest that arts education has benefited from the involvement (financial and other) of a number of institutions/groups/organizations. Contrary to the belief that the provision of arts education is a core responsibility of education systems, it appears that in practice a large number of non-education related government and non-government organisations directly contribute to arts education. While central government plays a major role in supporting arts education in 83% of countries, industry (63%), charities and foundations (67%) and individuals (63%) all perform foremost roles in arts education. International organisations (54%), galleries (42%) and broadcasters (46%) are also highly significant contributors to arts education. Trade unions are also involved in 20% of countries. Given the diversity of organisations involved, what is clear from the data is that, to be able to deliver arts education programmes within schools, the support of a number of institutions is required. It is therefore apparent that while implementation of arts policy begins with central government, it also needs the support of a number of non-government (NGOs) and cultural bodies. This makes the process of implementation more complex, but may add to the potential richness of the partnerships formed and enhance the quality of arts education provisions (see Table 2).

Table 2: Contributors and supporting institutions

Central Government	83
Foundations	67
Industry	63
Individuals	63
International organizations	54
Broadcasters	46
Galleries	42
Churches and Religious Org.	38
Trade Unions	21
No answer/invalid/illegible	11
Please provide examples (insert text)	0

The respondents were permitted to indicate multiple responses hence the percentages are not cumulative.

The general situation appears to be that central government provides the basic materials and support for arts education but that, to create quality programmes, additional support is needed from galleries, foundations, industry, NGOs and individuals. This seems to be the case regardless of the status of economic development of the country. Of particular significance, there appears to be a major disparity between the essential role played by a number of organisations and individuals outside the government – and particularly outside the education sector – in ensuring provisions of arts experiences within education. It could be argued that this crucial role has been generally overlooked. This is apparent in examination of the people responsible for policy and planning in arts education (see next section) where only negligible attention is given to the views of the diversity of funding and support partners. It could be argued that many seemingly 'outside' organisations are happy to fund arts education but remain as relatively silent partners. An alternative explanation may be that government bodies, and in particular education authorities – fail to acknowledge the highly significant impact of outside agencies within the provision of arts education within schools and therefore do not consult them in relation to arts policy.

There were several national systems where there was a strong and direct link between central government policy, curriculum and implementation – notably in Afghanistan and Singapore. In the former, arts education (though predominantly fine arts and craft) is compulsory through to the year 9 level and there are specific curriculum written for particular art and craft forms and the "subject is taught according to the rules and regulations and according to the curriculum provided". This notwithstanding, the problems of scarcity of resources, lack of faculties and the impact of war and hardship negatively impact on the way classroom policy can be enacted.

In smaller countries, such as the Republic of the Maldives, the focus of arts education has been on the development of resources to ensure implementation is supported to occur. For example, the development of an arts library and an online arts-related resources website have been designed to attempt to enhance the use of local resources and to encourage greater knowledge bases and foster artistic development. In other examples, smaller countries have made alliances with other countries to build and extend their artistic provisions. For example, the Cook Islands, in the South Pacific link closely with both Australia and New Zealand to add to their traditional arts practices. In these smaller systems, good policy and implementation at the coalface may be more directly associated with the passion and enthusiasm of a few individuals.

In Singapore, a national move to build greater creativity in education has been backed by the development and application of resources, changes to assessment, teacher professional development and teacher incentives. This has meant that there has been a relatively quick adoption of centralised policy.

There is a perception in many countries that funds from foundations and individuals tend to go to performance groups and cultural events and that it is difficult for arts education to compete for these funds. In particular, in many cases, funding from non-education government and non-government agencies goes directly to provide access to in-school or external performances or exhibitions in a one-off or isolated fashion. For example, within Denmark, cultural funding tagged for arts education may primarily be used to support performances and artists within schools, or educational programmes within cultural institutions. These programmes may or may not lead directly to an arts-rich education or ensure quality arts education experiences for children. As such, this funding is rarely viewed as being part of the overall strategic planning for arts education and may be tokenistic, ineffectual or – at the least – poorly capitalised within the framework of quality education. It is also acknowledged that partnerships with a range of NGOs provide more than financial resources. This is apparent in this comment from Canada.

> I think arts education does and can benefit from a raft of sources for entirely different reasons. Sometimes it is purely financial, other times it is by making available facilities or volunteers, or offering mentorship and internship programmes. Benefits to arts education have also been derived from an increasing demand for creative workforces, and an increasing demand for creative communities which would attract the businesses (thereby increasing municipal tax bases) that would employ the creative workforces.

Implied within this comment is the reciprocity of support for arts education. This has been echoed in examples of industry support for arts education that has resulted in significant benefits for both education and the industry partner. The Arts-in-Education programme in China was an initiative that involved artists and arts organisations working closely with teachers in the formal curriculum of the participating schools. It was organised by the *Hong Kong Arts Development Council (HKADC)* in collaboration with both the *Curriculum Development Institute of the Education and Manpower Bureau (EMB)* and the *Creative Arts Department of the Hong Kong Institute of Education (HKIEd)*. In order for the programme to proceed this three-year programme (2000-2003) received funding amounting to a total of four million Hong Kong dollars, donated by the *Hong Kong Bank Foundation*. The value of such partnerships was crucial to enable the programme to occur:

> With funding from the Hong Kong Bank Foundation, the three-year Arts-in-Education (AiE) programme (2000-2004) was jointly organised by the Arts Development Council (ADC), the Education and Manpower Bureau (EMB) and the Hong Kong Institute of Education. By pooling together the efforts of schools and artists, the AiE project aims at developing and enhancing the existing arts education system. The scheme tries to explore feasible and innovative ways of integrating the arts with other subjects in the formal school curricula so as to enhance the quality of both teaching and learning.

Qualitative comments suggest there is the sometimes problematic split between arts/cultural funding and education funding. There were also conflicts between local and central government. The general feeling was that local funding and a combination of arts and education funding was most likely to provide a solid fiscal base for quality arts education. In this example from the *State Pedagogical Institute* in Slovakia the combination of funding and other support from partners including galleries and museums, not only builds the feasibility of arts programmes, but also ensure that they are more pertinent to the needs of the 21st century. It is suggested that:

> The new concept of the subject – art teaching – is designed to enable its upgrading, in terms of primary education, from its "supplementary" position (i.e. of a subject that follows only partial aesthetic-educational objectives) into the position of a subject that fulfils a comprehensive (educational and training) mission and substantially participates in the development and shaping the personality of the student.

> The new concept of art teaching emancipates cognition of the traditional graphic and plastic arts disciplines and mediums, along with the disciplines and mediums brought about by 20th century art. It provides space to the acquisition of knowledge in the fields of visual culture – architecture and film. Also, it enables incorporating into the tuition programme the erudition and artistic processing of regional tradition, while considering active cooperation with museums and galleries, depending on specific conditions of the schools.

Compounding the challenges of the complex structure of implementation for arts-rich education, in addition to the role of external and cultural agencies, the education system itself may have both public and private sectors responsible for varying degrees of compliance with policy. For example, in Australia, public, private and religious schools operate at a state-based level to deliver policy and are covered by varying degrees of control in this process. In the USA local school governance boards and states may determine the degree of obligation of policy adoption. In Bangladesh both public and private sectors are responsible to ensure arts education is delivered. In this country, the split between the public and private systems is further complicated by the fact that the visual arts and crafts tend to be largely delivered through the public systems whereas the performing arts are more likely to be an additional provision delivered through the private system. Similarly in China, calligraphy is likely to be delivered through the state run system whereas the performing arts may be optional external provisions delivered through largely private sector providers.

The role of UNESCO, development banks and art endowments has been particularly vital in supporting arts education especially in the economically less-affluent countries. For example, diplomatic donations assisted arts education programmes in the Republic of Seychelles; UNESCO sponsored teacher training in the PEACE programme in Barbados, and; technical and financial support was received from the Inter-American Development bank and the British Council for arts education in Colombia.

Responsibilities for arts education policy

- Those who are responsible for the deliver of arts education have limited input into arts education policy
- Decentralised education and arts authorities influence policy implementation
- Central government and schools are responsible for arts education policy

Primarily, government and schools are jointly responsible for education policy as described in curricula. While schools were seen to be at the coalface of administering arts education, teachers, artists and children were rarely consulted in relation to the development of arts education policy. It was apparent that those who are responsible for the deliver of arts education have limited input into arts education policy and that attempts to influence arts education policy need to be directed at decentralised authorities.

Given the multi choice form of the survey, the respondents were able to identify multiple levels of responsibility in relation to arts education. It is consistent across the majority of cases (70%) that central government is responsible for the formulation of arts education policy. All other things being equal, we would expect the countries with a higher level of administrative decentralization and devolution of responsibilities (such as federal states like, USA, Canada and Australia) would be less likely to have centrally formulated arts curricula. Conversely it could be expected that unitary states (such as the Netherlands and the Nordic countries) have centrally generated curricula. This seemingly neat distinction is not evident in the findings. What is evident in the findings, however, is that the schools themselves have an equally large influence on the formulation of arts education policy (77%). This is a significant finding as previous attempts to influence arts policy have generally been directed at central level policy makers, and not at the decentralized level, that is, the schools. It is of note that the influence of schools is higher than that of local education authorities (50%). It would appear that school-based decisions are more important than state or provincial governments (54%), where these exist.

While the schools have influence over the formulation of arts education policy, it is of note, that individual teacher have relatively limited responsibility for the formulation of arts education policy (46%). This means that those at the coalface of delivering arts education policy are not directly responsible for its formulation. Nor are the users of arts education, that is the children (8%) and the parents (19%), consulted in relation to policy decisions. In fact in some countries there is a perception that parents and students place a low importance rating on the arts. For example in Tonga it is claimed that 98% of parents and children rated arts education of being of low importance. Conversely, in other countries such as Tuvalu, UK and Australia it has been parents and children demanding the arts education within their children's schools.

Despite intentions to involve communities more directly in arts education, the findings suggest that this trend has not been converted into greater levels of responsibility (only 27% of respondents identified the community as having a responsibility). Similarly, the trend for greater connection between arts education in schools and practicing artists has not translated into greater responsibility for the latter group (12% for artists) (see Table 3).

Table 3:   Policy makers (percentages)

Central government	77
School based decisions	77
State and Provincial Government	54
Local Education Authorities	50
Teachers	46
Community	27
Parents	19
Artists	12
Children	8
No answer/invalid/illegible	6
Other	0

The respondents were permitted to indicate multiple responses hence the percentages are not cumulative.

From the quantitative survey it is evident that both central government and the schools are responsible for art education. This finding needs to be complemented by the qualitative comments that indicate that a host of other bodies are responsible for the formulation of arts education. These include, art education organizations (professional associations, advocacy groups and the like), non-government organizations, arts organizations (including theatres and museums), academic researchers and tertiary education and the private sector. This multiplicity of different groups, individuals and organizations adds to the complexity of formulating and implementing arts education.

The place of arts education in the curriculum

- Arts education is part of education policy in most countries.
- There is considerable difference between what is mandated in a country and the nature and quality of the arts education programme the children in schools actually receive.

Arts education is a compulsory part of school education in 84% of countries. Within these countries, 94% of the respondents stated that arts education was taught as a freestanding subject in its own right (though the nature of what this entails is more fully understood by reading the previous section on 'what is art education'). Of those countries where arts education is a compulsory part of general education, 78% examine or assess arts learning, while 18% of countries do not examine arts education (see Tables 4 and 5).

Table 4:   Percentage of countries where Arts Education is Mandated/
            Compulsory part of the curriculum

Arts education mandated	84
Arts education not mandated	16
No answer/invalid/illegible	7
Don't Know	0
Total	100

Cumulative percentages

Table 5:   Percentage of countries where Arts Education is examined

Arts education examined/assessed	78
Arts education not examined/assessed	17
No answer/invalid/illegible	15
Don't Know	4
Total	100

Cumulative percentages

Conversely, some countries had no arts education policy. The small Pacific country of Tuvalu has no standard art curriculum or syllabus, but embedded within their ideas of education is the need for a child to have an "open mind" and to "build the skills for a bright future". While this would not statistically appear as the inclusion of arts policy, arts education is one of the learning areas that occur within a Tuvalu curriculum. Driven by the strong support from the children themselves, Tuvaluan people make sure that "arts education flourishes throughout Tuvalu".

On average 176 hours per year in primary schools and an average of 165 hours per year in secondary schools were spent on arts education. It should be noted that the standard deviation (SD) of this figure was considerable. In non-technical terms, the figures differ significantly from the statistical mean. It would thus appear to makes little sense to focus on the statistical average. A closer look at the data, however, reveals that the considerable differences are largely due to significant out-layers, most notably Finland. In this country, arts education account for 80 percent of the teaching time. Not because they teach arts to the exclusion of all other subjects, but because all subjects are taught through what this book terms *education through the arts*. The reason for this is, probably, culture specific (also see later section that argues the distinction between integrated and specialized curricula).

Conversely, several countries had limited or no specific times dedicated to arts education. Within this data set, several countries indicated a high level of variation between the times spent on arts education. For example, within the United States of America (USA) there is a, "wild variation from school to school and community to community, with some schools receiving almost no arts education whatsoever and where it does exist, it is typically for 40-minute periods". The *National Center for Education Statistics of the U.S. Department of Education* (The National Center for Education Statistics of the U.S. Department of Education, 2000) in the 1999-2000 school year found that arts education received 46 hours per year in public elementary and 44 hours within secondary schools.

A number of survey respondents also identified the variation between the 'official' requirement, in terms of the preferred policy statement and what was occurring in practice. This seemed to be the case in a variety of countries regardless of their economic status. For example, in Australia, arts education is mandated in all systems and was generally given specific allocated time in the curricula in the secondary school, but within the primary school the enactment of this mandated time was likely to be highly dependent upon the schools and the teacher within the schools.

Several of the countries also raised the issue of quality as being an important proviso in the amount of art education children receive. While the question specifically asked for an amount of time, several respondents acknowledged that measuring time was not always a good indication of the extensiveness of arts education. This discrepancy is effectively underlined by the respondents from Colombia who state:

> Although the *Law of Education* in Colombia acknowledges the importance of artistic education, and includes it as a mandatory area in the curriculum, it leaves it up to the autonomy of each school to determine the time devoted to and the emphasis placed upon art education. The *Institutional Education Project (PEI)* designed and

implemented by each school determines time and emphasis in art education. However, experience shows that only very few schools lay considerable weight on art education.

In Japan, the *Fundamental Law of Education (1947)* determines that every child receives an equal access to education. This law has been further developed to include the *Fundamental Law for the Promotion of Arts and Culture (2001)* that stipulates that education institutions, including schools, must improve education related to culture and arts. This means that there are mandated courses of study and standard hours for arts education across primary and secondary school. This mandated syllabus includes art, craft, music, life and environment studies and a range of optional electives. It also provides a directive for integrated study. For example, a child in the first year of primary school would experience around 300 hours per year (or roughly 6 hours per week). In the final compulsory years of arts education (secondary school, year 9) a child would receive approximately 140 hours per year as a core and up to an additional 165 hours as possible electives.

The figures on amount of time given to arts education need to be carefully examined as there was not only a discrepancy between what was mandated and what was actual, but also between the arts education that occurred within the school day (that is, as a key part of the curriculum) and that which occurred outside the school day in optional sessions, generally deemed to be more recreational than educationally based. Having said this though, in many cases, it appeared that the 'out of school provisions' were well-organized and operated effectively. For example in Spain the *'activities artisticas'* appear to be a substantial source of arts education operated in the afternoon, after formal school.

There is also the distinction between core compulsory units (generally in primary school and the early years of high school) and the provision of elective subjects (generally in senior secondary school). Education *in the arts* is more likely at secondary level while integrated education *through the arts* is more common at the elementary school level. This issue is described in more detail in a later section.

Arts education policy

- Effective arts education can inform broader arts and cultural policy.
- The media can benefit arts advocacy.
- Sustained evaluation and monitoring of arts education enhances the ability to influence government policy.

Results from the survey indicate that some form of art education policy exists in 84% of countries, but the results of the qualitative data suggest that there is a gap between the existence of policy at the national level and the way it is converted into pragmatic changes at the classroom level. The data suggests that in 55% of countries, successful art programmes had led to strategies that impacted on national arts education policy. However in 46% of countries – despite successful examples of art programmes existing within these countries – there had been little or no change more broadly to arts education or general education policy.

Within this area there are several key findings. Firstly, effective arts education can inform broader arts and cultural policy beyond the classroom. The influence of arts education on broader arts and cultural policy seems to have emerged from closer links between arts and education authorities. For example, in Canada there has been a trend in recent years for more collaboration between Ministries of Education and Culture, educators and artists.

Conversely, effective cultural policy may in fact lead to better arts education in schools. This is the case in Germany where the arts policy of the city of Munich is influenced by the positive effects of cultural and arts education projects for children and youth. Similarly, in the following case from Canada, advocacy by school students led to the retention of arts education within a local school area, according to the Canadian respondent who reported: "I would say that at the municipal level, arts students can engage in civic dialogue about arts policy. I once had a grade 11 class give a deposition to city council to continue the current level of arts funding."

It was also acknowledged that arts and cultural authorities have in recent years shown a greater interest in arts education policy and practices. In the Netherlands it was noted that "positive changes in arts policy have contributed to arts education projects" and that "arts policy makers have shown an increased interest in arts education."

While many countries reported that arts and education authorities were working more closely together, in some countries, such as Austria, there were strict divisions between arts and education authorities and it was stated that this adversely impacted on the implementation of arts education policy.

According to the survey, organisations such as *Americans for the Arts* and *The Arts Education Partnership* in the USA have actively lobbied at the national level for the inclusion of arts education in general policy. While this has been successful in some school districts, other States have no provision for arts education, such as in California. This can be contrasted to more centralised systems of educational governance, where centrally driven policy has had a substantial impact on art education provisions. For example, in Singapore the *National Arts Council's Arts Education Programme (NAC-AEP)* that was established since 1993 has created a significant impact in arts policy where it was considered that: "Over the years, there has been a growing demand from schools for arts education programmes and a number of programmes are being offered by the increased number of artists and arts groups." While Singapore is an example of a quite centralised education system, it was also noted that the support of the school principal was vital to building quality arts programmes. For example, despite the national policy, one school in Singapore noted that up until 3 years ago, there had been only *ad hoc* arts programmes and most of the arts events involved only the performing CCA groups (basically, Dance Club, Band and Choir). However, "when the new Principal took over leadership, policy was changed to have arts enrichment programme incorporated into curriculum time." This, and other similar findings, point to the need for both top-down and a bottom-up approaches to policy implementation in the arts.

Conversely, some countries had taken considerable steps at the national level to ensure full implementation of arts policy. For example, within Thailand a number of enacted arts policies including the *National Scheme of Education, Religion Art and Culture (2002-2016)* are part of a larger strategic plan that includes detailed implementation and guidance strategies aimed at ensuring wide scale classroom reform at the national and local level. However, the while such a clearly articulated plan exists, there is no designated agency directly responsible for evaluating the implementation or impact of this programme in Thailand and this is likely to limit its widespread adoption.

Another issue highlighted was the role of the media in promoting 'good news stories' of successful arts education programmes. These serve to draw attention to the value of the arts and assist in persuading policy makers and local education authorities to include a greater focus on art education. For instance, in Canada and Australia positive media coverage of successful arts education programmes had led to the inclusion of more arts education within the curriculum. This was also noted in Finland where media attention encouraged greater inclusion of arts education, but the Finish respondents cautioned that it should not be necessary to gain media attention before arts education was on the policy agenda. There was also concern in Canada that while media attention may highlight effective arts in education programmes, there was also a sense that media coverage also highlighted arts education deficiencies in other communities and that it was the local agenda which has the larger impact on arts policy than media coverage. This issue has been described as follows:

> I've seen growing movement in this area [media coverage of the arts in education] of late, more collaboration between Ministries of Education and Culture, educators and artists. This may be triggered by some good-news arts education projects, but my sense is that a few good-news projects only highlight deficiencies in other communities and that it is the communities'/municipalities' agenda which having the larger impact on arts policy.

The role of sustained evaluation and monitoring appears to be more significant than the impact of the media and the lobbying organisations in promoting policy changes. In England self-evaluation is a requirement of all arts education projects funded. The system of monitoring is detailed and rigorous, as evidenced in this description:

> We have developed Partnerships for Learning (Woolf, 1999), a guide to evaluating arts education projects to aid with this [programme evaluation]. The Arts Council selects many of these project evaluations to aid with the spending review case for investment by government. Where there are major national programmes we deliver on behalf of government these are evaluated and help to influence policy. Two of our projects – Creative Partnerships and the Arts and Education Interface – looks at impact of arts education projects in many areas and these are intended to inform both arts and education policy development.

There is a need for more detailed rigorous evaluation and monitoring studies of arts education programmes so that the findings from these studies can be used to inform policy makers. It is also apparent that arts education projects frequently suffer from inadequate longevity. Effective programmes may be short-term and lack sustained funding. This means that the impact of these programmes on policy is reduced. Conversely, where effective arts education has been part of education for a sustained time, there is clear evidence that this becomes acculturated and more readily accepted as part of education policy. This process of building a culture of support for the arts within education is apparent within the Senegalese example:

> Arts Education has existed for a long time in Senegal and has largely contributed to the education of the artists and the public. Thus, any policy aiming at the promotion of arts benefits – directly or indirectly – is influenced by this well protected heritage. Besides, teachers and artists who have received this formation [quality arts education] are now top executives in the cultural and academic administration. This enables them to take part to the decision-making along with the highest Governmental Authorities.

It should be acknowledged, that while this section has been addressing the challenges of implementing arts education policy and the impact of arts education both on cultural policy and general education policy, many countries who responded to the survey still do not have any formal arts education policy. Allied to the lack of arts education policy is the often precarious relationship between provisions within the school (as part of the formal education policy) and provisions outside the school (seen more as an optional part of the informal policy). While many non-formal and out-of-school programmes appear to be of high quality and successful there is a caution about the arts being marginalised to the non-formal sector. For example, while excellent arts programmes exist in China within the after school, non-formal sector, the formal curriculum is very "economically driven" and "arts education is still being marginalised a lot." This division between the formal and informal sectors is exacerbated by divisions between the authorities responsible for school education and those responsible for community provisions. The complexity of this is highlighted in this example from Finland:

> The Ministry of Education is divided into an Educational Division (Minister of Education) and the Cultural Division (the Minister of Culture). The Cultural Division is very active in supporting arts education out of school, but the State Government made a cut in arts lessons when we got a new core curriculum. We have a good out-of-school arts education system, but only 12% of the children between 7 and 18 are able to take part in it. The National Board of Education has given to all art forms core curricula for two interest profiles, a general one and an extensive one. So the problem is that art education depends on the interest of families, when the compulsory school does not have the possibility to give good basic arts education any more.

Visual musical notations. Linking learning across the curriculum in an expressive way. (Education and Arts Partnership Initiative, Australia). Photograph courtesy of the author.

Furthermore, due to the rapidly changing society, many education systems are undergoing quite radical reform at all levels. While the urgent need to examine the validity of current education provisions in terms of preparing children for the 21st century has frequently provided a pathway for the arts to adopt a more central position within education, in some instances, this reform process has led to the devaluing of the arts, especially education in the arts (as opposed to education through the arts). In New Zealand a period of unprecedented educational reform resulted in a greatly enhanced arts and cultural component as core to current and future education requirements. The wider acknowledgement of the need for dual curriculum models to cater for the needs of Maori and other learners and radical changes to assessment regimes has led directly to an arts strategy that embeds dance, drama, visual arts and music into New Zealand education. Conversely curriculum reforms in Nepal have seen the over-theorisation of arts education and the enveloping of arts education under and framework of health and physical education.

The role of arts education policy in general education policy

- The importance of the arts within education policy is under rated.
- A large gulf exists between espoused policy in arts education and existing practices.
- Greater research is needed on the impact of arts-rich programmes on general education.

While arts education appears in the education policy in some form in most countries, the arts are generally not viewed as being an important part of general education policy. There appears to be a large gap between espoused policy in arts education and generally poor provisions experienced within classrooms.

The data indicate that general education policy largely ignores the arts or sees that arts as being marginalised. In 59% of cases general education policy did not acknowledge at all the contribution of arts education. This figure is interesting as earlier survey figures suggest that arts education is a compulsory part of education policy in 84% of cases. This deviation in the data is explained in part by the way the question was asked. The initial data asked for whether art education was part of the education policy for a country, while the latter question asked if arts education had impacted general education policy. In comparing the quantitative data with the qualitative comments, what becomes apparent is that while art education exists "in paper" in many countries, it is not valued and acknowledged within curriculum and the pragmatics of what occurs within the classroom. This was commonly identified problem across the responses from many countries.

This is very evident for example in the USA, where art education is listed as a core academic subject in the *No Child Left Behind Act (2002),* which is the reauthorization of the *Elementary and Secondary Education Act of 1965* and is included as part of education policy, but, according to the survey respondents, children within schools in many American states, such as California, receive little no formal arts education as part of the curriculum. The *National Center for Education Statistics (NCES)* conducts periodic surveys to determine the conditions of arts teaching and learning in grades K-12 in the USA. The most recent survey report, *Arts Education in Public Elementary and Secondary Schools: 1999-2000* found that provisions were dispersed and sporadic.

Similarly, despite extensively driven centralised policy to support the arts and creativity in schools, the Ministry of Education in Singapore has given "more autonomy to school principals and allowed them to creatively used their resources to reach their schools' goals and outcomes." While this has led to many excellent examples of arts education programmes being offered at the school level, it also means that children in some schools receive only limited arts education.

In a number of the countries surveyed, education policy either ignored arts education or arts education was marginalised by practices that are not conducive to the establishment of quality programmes. The impact of policy was a limiting factor is evident in this example from the Republic of Seychelles:

> Educational policy in practice is still based on an archaic divisive model ... opportunities for curiosity, lateral thinking, project based learning are very restricted by (1) mono-dimensional teaching methods, (2) overcrowded class-rooms, (3) poor or erratic supply of basic materials and (4) little or no student access to computer/IT equipment.

This example underlines the complexities of placing sustained arts education on the general education agenda, especially in a climate of limited resources. Even in economically advanced nations it has been difficult to position the arts in the educational agenda. Even in countries with excellent arts education programmes, such as those within Finland, economic imperatives mean that the arts are often marginalised within general education policy. The impact of economic constraints seems to be particularly felt within the arts sector as this quote from Finland suggests: "Nowadays the schools have less money and lessons/resources for the Arts than few years ago."

In the Netherlands this is very much the case where art is on the educational agenda but "in other European countries some careful steps were made, but we can not say anything about the influence of it. In some European countries this [arts education] is still not happening." This statement underlines a general, if tacit, educational

Carlos Mario Lema. Colombia, Plan Nacional Música para la convivencia. Photo courtesy of Monica Romero and Clarisa Ruiz.

prioritisation that places the arts at a disadvantage *vis-à-vis* such subjects as mathematics, science and literacy. In times of economic constraint, cuts within arts programmes are more common place than within other subjects.

Appreciation of the value of arts within the general education policies of a country seems to be a classic case of what is termed *path-dependency*, whereby previous experiences at the local level (generally schools) generate an understanding of the value of arts-rich education. However, these experiences are not adequately communicated to – appreciated by – the 'powers that be' within educational hierarchy where arts policies tend to be absent, or tokenistic. This point is emphasised in the response from Austria that suggests that, "Maybe there has been some influence on education policy within individual school locations but not structurally."

The respondents from Spain expanded the debate about the influence of art education on general education policy by suggesting that art and cultural education is no longer valued by the family and community and this is being reflected in the lack of value given to arts education within schools. In Spain it was suggested that:

> The respect for the external thing, the novel thing, the foreign thing, the cultural thing, has been lost. And this is not just due to the schools and academies. Culture should begin in the breast of the family, and the present situation has made that culture disappear.

While the focus of this section has been on school education policy, it is also significant that several responding countries highlighted higher education policy as being a contributing factor to the success or otherwise of arts education policy. For instance, in Barbados, the establishment of creative arts courses within universities was seen as a major positive step towards broader arts education policy and the development of sustained educational pathways in the arts. Examples from Colombia also point to the importance of support from cultural institutions to build recognition of the value of arts education within general education policy. In this example, the combined efforts of a number of agencies had resulted in significant increase in the status of the arts within general education policy:

> A recent movement of artists, teachers, government policy makers and experts in education has been developing strategies to stress the importance and value of arts and cultural education in learning. Examples of this movement that can be mentioned are *Proyecto RED de la Universidad Nacional, Proyecto de Investigación del IDEP de la Secretaría del Distrito Capital*. Also the Ministry of Culture recently conducted a seminar on Art Education Policies, and a permanent research team was created to continue the work started in the seminar. The principal aim of this research team is to design a public policy for this field of education taking as a starting point the articulation between non-formal and formal artistic education.

Finally, many of the respondents called for greater impact research to inform general education research. This call came particularly from the UK and Australia, where it was felt that substantial evaluative and monitoring studies would produce major policy and practice changes. This is exemplified through this case study from Australia, where an innovative approach to arts education with indigenous children had received considerable media and public attention for its successes:

Although the following projects/programmes have considerable profile in the Northern Territory education sector and also nationally, I believe the influence upon positive changes in education policy is unlikely at this stage. The Education Department and other jurisdictions are actively seeking evidence of the impact ofalternative approaches to indigenous education and boys' education. This presents an opportunity for arts-based approaches to be taken up, trialled and evaluated. To date the Education and the Arts Partnership Initiative funded by the Australia Council for the Arts is the only project that has rigorously evaluated the impact of arts education upon students' literacy and numeracy outcomes, the use of arts-based assessment materials and processes, and the impact of an arts-based model of professional learning for teachers in schools.

Distinction between education in the arts and education through the art

- There is a clear distinction between education in the arts and education through the arts.
- These should be considered in a complementary but separate manner when considering arts education policy and practices.

Distinction needs to be made in interpretation of the figures on amount of time spent between dedicated arts education (that is education in the arts) and integrated arts education (that is, education through the arts). The data tends to indicate that education in the arts is more likely at secondary level while integrated education through the arts is more common at the elementary school level. It is not the purposes of this report to suggest which of these is better, but rather to indicate that the presence of integrated arts curricula can serve to bias the data, particularly when a large amount of the time notionally recorded as 'arts education' may in fact be teaching other subjects through art. For example, Finland, who appeared to have by far the highest amount of arts education, in excess of 300 hours in primary school, acknowledged that this figure was derived from both specialist and integrated arts education, in so far as;

> Usually schools have all their compulsory arts education before the eight class and after that it is possible for pupils to choose optional courses not only in visual arts and music but also sometimes in theatre and dance. Usually these two subjects are a part of mother tongue and physical education (classes 1-6). Arts education should be integrated in all curriculum subjects.

A major finding of the research has been that there are well-researched and documented impacts of arts-rich education. As the quote from Senegal suggest, these fall under two distinct aspects:

> Before answering the survey, I would like to share with the coordinators the idea of Arts Education as a double dimension process – 'Education to the Arts' and 'Education by the Arts'. Thus it places the cultural coherence of the child at the heart of any educational strategy. Moreover, this vision increases the value of all the disciplines and processes that have always been used by the communities – according to their own culture – to mould children's identity through their emotional and cognitive predispositions. Hence the importance too of the social dimension of Arts Education which protects poor children from being marginalized from the educational system. (Alioune Badiane, Ministry for Culture and Heritage, Senegal 2004)

Education in the arts can be described as being sustained and systematic learning in the skills, ways of thinking and presentation of each of the art forms – dancing, visual arts, music, drama – produces impacts in terms of improved attitudes to school and learning, enhanced cultural identity and sense of personal satisfaction and well-being. Concurrently, education which uses creative and artistic pedagogies to teach all curricula – education through the arts – enhances overall academic attainment, reduces school disaffection and promotes positive cognitive transfer. These benefits are only accrued where there were provisions of quality programmes. Poor quality programmes, were seen to actively inhibit the benefits apparent in good quality programmes.

This is an important finding as previous studies have tended to confuse these areas or see these two distinct areas as being one. It is important to note, that for children to maximise their educational potential, both approaches are needed. Equally, it is of significance that high quality education where there is the greatest impact at all levels – child, learning environment and community – is achieved where excellent programmes exist both in the arts and through artistic approaches, such as in case study examples from Canada, Australia, United Kingdom, Finland, Slovakia and others. *Education in the arts* and *education through the arts*, while distinct, are interdependent and it should not be assumed that it is possible to adopt one or the other to achieve the totality of positive impacts on the child's educational realization.

Chapter 5:
Arts education in practice

Introduction

This chapter examines the issues surrounding the enactment of arts education in practice. The qualities of accomplished arts practices become apparent and are most likely to be revealed, at least in part, in the practices within education. The research indicated that while advocacy to include arts as part of education policy has largely been successful, this has not led to wide scale implementation of quality arts programmes at the school level.

This global research – by its very nature – revealed that educational systems are deeply embedded in cultural and nation specific contexts. This is especially the case as regards education in the arts. More than any other subject, the arts (itself a broad category) reflect unique cultural circumstances, and consequently, so does the teaching of the subject.

This chapter examines in detail the implementation and delivery of arts education within schools and outlines the nature of quality arts programmes. As teachers play such a pivotal role in the provision of arts education delivery, special attention is paid to issues of teacher training, including in-service professional development.

The arts learning environment

- Arts education tends to be poorly resourced compared to other areas of general education
- Motivated, creative staff can compensate for under resourced programmes to produce quality outcomes

While the problems in arts education go beyond physical constraints within the classroom, the environment in which teachers must administer their arts education programmes compounds the difficulties faced in the implementation of quality art programmes. Teachers are faced with the dilemma of reconciling curriculum decision-making with the realities of contextual factors such as lack of time, space and resources. Despite this, arts educators become realists within the framework of this act of reconciliation. As Ellis (1954: 88) notes: "Just as a sculptor works in the reality of limestone or walrus-ivory or teak, the art educator has his [sic] realities... these conditions, provoke, prevent, permit or invite him [sic] in his [sic] work." This is certainly evident in the case studies where a lack of resources – while not in itself a desirable state – did not limit the ability to conduct quality arts programmes.

Art programmes were able to operate effectively with children sitting on the dirt, in dilapidated old cinemas and where paper was a luxury. Yet the ingenuity of artists and teachers should not be taken as an excuse for under funding the arts within general education.

In almost every research case study, lack of funds, inadequate resources, insufficient dedicated time and rigid structures were considered to be factors that limited the success of an arts-rich programme. This was particularly evident in economically developing countries where the demands on educational funds were considerable and the arts were often the most adversely effected in terms of limited funds. For example in Bangladesh the scarcity of funds meant that arts education had to operate within a climate of inadequate materials, shortage of qualified teachers and acute funding shortfalls. These economic problems were not limited to just the arts education provisions. In Kyrgyzstan for example, challenges of a large foreign debt, low teacher salaries and status and limitations of resources and technology impacted on all education but were seen to be a limiting factor in more extensive adoption of arts education provisions.

Chia (1995: 6) writes the following comment in relation to teaching conditions in Singapore, "The preparation of generalist art teachers for primary classes although reasonable, cannot ever be sufficient when these young teachers encounter a typical situation as the one described." The situation described is one of low educational priority for arts; poor valuing of arts by senior school personnel, a lack of teacher training in the arts, the arts viewed as a pastime rather than an academic endeavour, and inadequate teaching of arts skills and appreciation. Eisner (1999: 18) comments:

> If those who teach the arts are doing about as well as can be expected in the situation in which they find themselves, and if the results of their work fall short of our collective aspirations, how can we expect more without a substantial change in the resources provided to those who teach the arts?

Responsibilities for delivery of arts education programmes

- Teachers are largely responsible for teaching arts education
- "Teachers" of arts education include both generalist and specialist educators, artists, and the members of community
- Teachers generally receive little or no specific arts education training
- Artists and the community are taking an increasing role in the teaching of arts education

Of the 46% of arts education, which is delivered by teachers, 85% are generalist teachers, i.e. teachers who teach a variety of subjects (See Table 7). This is particularly the case in the primary school, where the number of specialist teachers is relatively low. But what does generalist mean in this context? The fundamental question is how much training these have received. The figures show that 54% of the generalist teachers have received less than 3 months or no arts education training. While the figure for more than 3 months training is 49%. Previous studies of generalist teacher education in the arts would suggest that this figure may be inflated, with some countries counting general teacher education within the calculation of specific arts training. Despite this, with more than half of the generalist teachers receiving almost no training in arts education, and yet being largely responsible for the delivery of arts education, there is need for significant concern.

Within the secondary sector, there are a higher proportion of specialist teachers, i.e. teachers who predominately teach arts disciplines (81%). The teacher education for specialist art teachers seems to be better with 80% receiving more than one year of training (See Table 7). However, there is a concern that even within this specialist group, 15% of teachers receive less than 3 months of no arts education training (see Table 8).

Table 7:   Responsibility for teaching arts education

Generalist teachers	85
Specialist teachers	81
Artists	56
Parents	19
Community	19
Others (Healthcare workers, children, etc.).	33

Cumulative percentages

Table 8 shows that the majority of art teaching in primary schools is done by generalist teachers with limited art training and, correspondingly, with limited confidence in their personal arts ability. In commenting on the quality of primary art teachers in Australian schools, Duncum (1999: 15) makes this observation:

> Few generalist teachers know much about art, and consequently what many do is trivial. At Easter, for example, adult drawings of rabbits are commonly photocopies, children colour-in the photocopies and use cotton wool to make cute fluffy tails. Many generalists feel that if they can't draw, they can't teach art. Feeling they cannot teach skills, what they do in art is to explore numerous materials, or one material in numerous ways.

Table 8:   Amount of training for specialist and generalist teachers (%)

Generalist Teachers	85	
No training		18
Less than 3 months training		36
3-12 months training		9
More than 1 year training		36
No answer/invalid/illegible (training only)		4
No answer/invalid/illegible (whole question)	15	
Total	100	
Specialist Teachers	81	
No training		10
Less than 3 months training		5
3-12 months training		5
More than 1 year training		80
No answer/invalid/illegible (training only)		9
No answer/invalid/illegible (whole question)	19	
Total	100	

Cumulative percentages. Generalist teachers are defined as those who teach arts education and other subjects. Specialist teachers are those who only teach arts subjects.

This comment is echoed by Eisner (1999:17) who claims that, "we are expecting teachers to teach what they do not know and often do not love." Conversely, a trend indicated in the data that has not generally been considered in relation to the delivery of arts-rich education is that artists are increasingly taking a role in the delivery of arts education (56%). This figure is interesting given that data from the previous chapter on policy responsibility shows that artists are rarely involved in the formulation of policy (12%) but are quite significant players in the deliver of the arts. This would indicate a need to more directly involve input from artists in arts education policy design. The data suggests that artists are reasonably well-trained (with 54% having more than a year arts training). Once again, this figure needs to be interpreted with care as it is unclear whether the training indicated by each country includes general training as an artist (e.g. a fine arts degree) or specific arts education training. Given this caveat, it is still significant that of the artists actively teaching arts education in the schools, 31% receive less than 3 months or no arts education training. If the involvement of artists within arts education is to be encouraged, consideration needs to be given to the training of artists whose practice will largely be conducted within an educational context. Such professional development would need to be handled with care as the intention would be to give artists a broader understanding of the educational context, but not acculturate them into being pseudo 'teachers'. Clearly apparent within the case studies is the idea that artists bring something unique and valuable to arts-rich education and that this would be lost if they were to resemble too closely the formal teaching staff.

The lack of quality and qualified teachers impinges directly on the quality of arts education received by the child in the classroom. As is eloquently concluded within Nepal "A good class of art and craft depends on teachers themselves." The vital role played by passionate and committed teachers in ensuring quality arts-rich education is apparent in all national systems and is the single most important determining factor effecting coalface quality.

In the Irish programme, *"Artformations"* the partnership between artist and educators enhanced the professional capacities of both groups. The programme acknowledged that both artists and teachers have particular expertise. In particular, it was felt that the expertise of the teacher could be shared with the artists in terms of stages of learning development, school structures and classroom management.

Furthermore, many countries have instigated large scale curriculum and policy reform to place the arts in a more central position within education but these initiatives have largely been unsuccessful without adequate pre-service and inservice professional development. For example, within Mongolia detailed arts standards have been developed and applied but "a lack of training for teachers in the implementation of the new standards" means that in many instances the arts education a child receives has changed very little. Conversely, as stated previously, in countries where policy change has been supported by teacher training, such as in Colombia, major advances have been able to be made in a relatively short timeframe.

The community also plays an important role in the delivery of arts education programmes (19%). Of the community engaged in arts education, 75% receive no training. The qualitative comments suggest that levels of arts education are generally inadequate. For example, a comment from Australia suggests, "My observation is that most people delivering some form of music education to students in the Northern Territory have little or no formal training as instrumentalists or music educators." Similarly, the Canadian response indicates that, while data on levels and quality of teacher education is not fully available, there is the general belief that levels of training are "inadequate". In the Seychelles, the issue of training is a particular problem, with many supply teachers receiving no training either in education or arts. Finland appears to have the most extensive arts education training (more than 5 years), but it is unclear from the data if this is art training or specific arts education training.

Given the importance of issues of teacher education within the provision of quality arts-rich programmes, it warrants a more detailed analysis of the issues surrounding teacher education. While within the scope of the research conducted, it was not intended to conduct a definitive examination of teacher education, the following section highlights in a general sense some for the concerns revealed through the case studies into the way in which a lack for skilled implementation staff inhibit the wider adoption for centrally driven arts policy within education. A note of caution at this point is that while the existence of arts and cultural aspects within general education policy is quite uniform across international boundaries, it is less clear the extent to which arts education is valued within the mindset. It is well-established in the implementation literature that blueprints, whitepapers, and mission-statements of espoused policies are not enough to ensure the delivery of quality policies. Public policies – whether in arts education or in general – rely on effective implementation structures, not simply on the training of the teachers. As a respondent from Nigeria suggests:

> It is not easy stating where curriculum implementation starts and ends. Does implementation start when teachers complete initial training or when teachers are re-trained for new programmes? Does implementation occur when arts education becomes embedded as a regular stage instead of being an experimental stage? Curriculum implementation is a complex process that deals with people with diverse views, ideas and backgrounds. Parents, students, teachers, producers of educational materials, subject associations and government are all directly involved in policy implementation. Policy implementation is also effected by the society and its culture. There is therefore the need to give attention to some of these social matters such as favouritism, public myth, rejection, local reputation, prejudice and behavioural instability in curriculum implementation. Government establishes curriculum but how far each school puts into action this curriculum depends on the Principal of the school who may not see art as important. The policy states that *National Certificate in Education* teachers teach in primary school but this is not the case in practice.

Comparative research in education has established that the most effective means of ensuring delivery of centrally enacted policies is by acknowledging the cross-pressures of the front-line staff and to develop structures that enable them to implement quality programmes (Elmore 1981). Simply adding another task to an already growing list is not a recipe for success.

Teacher education

- A review of teacher education in the arts is urgently needed
- Focused improvements in teacher education led directly to improved arts education in the classroom
- Inservice professional development is generally more effective in changing teacher attitudes to and skill levels in facilitating arts learning than preservice training
- A growing number of artists see their practice as existing in large part within an educational context and these artists require specific educational training

A review of teacher education is an urgent priority, especially in relation to the training received by generalist teachers and the minimum requirements for specialist arts teachers. It would also be valuable to examine in more detail the qualifications of different specialists across the various art forms. Allied with this, courses need to be developed to accommodate the growing demand for training for artists working primarily within the educational sector, as a place of professional practice.

One of the key issues needed to be overcome to more generally enhance the quality of arts-rich education is improved teacher education. The results of the survey indicate that while pre-service teacher education is important, the lessons learnt early in a teaching career are not being carried on into the classroom setting. Teacher education is often seen by students to be of little relevance, being overly abstract and theoretical (Brady, Segal et al. 1998). Any arts learning that occurs within pre service programmes tends to be decontextualised and characterised by individual competition for the best grades rather than collaborative learning strategies (Brady, Segal et al. 1998).

Condous (1999) writes of the need for teachers to be trained well if arts are to be taught well. Yet there are a number of limiting factors impacting upon the quality of art teacher education. Duncum (1999: 15) comments that the preservice teaching of primary generalists is considered the "black hole" of arts education. It is felt that literacy and numeracy training is given a far higher priority in teacher education than the arts. This view is summarised by Taylor (1986: 256) who writes:

> Because society sees and values the importance of numeracy and literacy skills, it expects its intending primary teachers to have obtained minimum qualification in these areas and they form an essential part of course content. Unfortunately, little consideration is given to the important part in our lives which is played by what might be termed visual literacy.

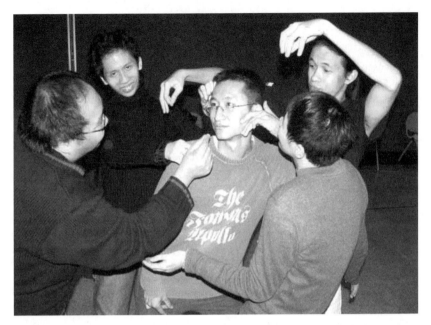

Human sculpture. The formation of 'special needs' arts educators through the integration of five distinct stories into inclusive dance-sculpture as preparation for creating pedagogies which celebrate difference and nurture democracy (Institute of Transformation, Hong Kong, 2005). Photo courtesy of Dan Baron Cohen.

This problem of the lack of time dedicated to art education, especially in generalist teacher training, is compounded by the lack of entering ability possessed by students. Holt (1997: 95) notes that students entering generalist primary teaching courses have little experience of the arts, although they are surrounded by examples of the arts in their everyday lives. Holt's (1997) survey of students entering primary teacher education reveals that the majority of students perceive the arts as having little value to the real world and as being unregarded and a pointless activity. Geahigan (1999) also comments that most of the students he encounters in arts classes in primary teacher education lack any entry points that would enable them to engage actively with artworks and offer sustained reflection about the arts.

Similar findings are noted in Nakamura's (1999: 10) study of sixty-four preservice Japanese generalist teachers. He found that primary teachers generally had:

- A difficulty explaining verbally what they thought and felt about art with shallow conversations that lack depth;
- A lack of confidence in their own ideas in relation to art;
- A tendency to remain with primary impressions of art, often feeling uncomfortable looking at art works analytically and understanding them rationally;

- A feeling that art should be enjoyed more with emotion rather than with inquiry;
- A difficulty having dialogues about art with other students; and,
- A lack of confidence in their own abilities.

Preservice primary teachers are required to gain competence across all discipline and curriculum areas and to have training in a number of non-curriculum specific fields, such as special education and child protection. As Wright (1989: 9) notes, teacher education has become, "a difficult if not impossible task to expect early primary teachers to gain competence in all curriculum areas." A fundamental dilemma for teacher educators is the question of what to include and what to omit given the time constraints that exist (Boughton 1999). Determining what knowledge is most important, the ways that it should be presented to students, as well as what is to be gained by students as a result of the educational experience, are key questions in arts education. Bresler (1995: 18) writes of this same dilemma in the American context, reflecting on, "a proliferation of values, differing with their view of what is worthwhile art knowledge, the organisation of learning opportunities, and suitable pedagogues for these learning opportunities." Given this view, the results of the survey would suggest that the focus of attention should be on quality inservice professional development partnerships rather than trying to concentrate reforms on an already overloaded preservice sector. There is a need to educate, rather than simply train arts teachers. Keifer-Boyd (1997) recommends a move away from the 'banking' concept of professional education, whereby doses of knowledge are seemingly 'deposited' into teachers. Instead, she suggests the metaphor of the 'midwife' where – through working together – teachers and artists are able to gently nurture and facilitate the bringing forth of knowledge and skills through research and critical inquiry.

Several countries instigated strategies aimed specifically at improving the level of qualification of arts educators. The results indicate that not only is there vast improvement in the quality of provision of arts education within schools, but more broadly, arts-based teaching pedagogy leads to enhanced creative and innovative approaches to teaching pedagogy across all disciplines. In Canada, many teachers opt for "additional qualifications" so they move ahead in their careers. Teachers regularly choose arts qualifications (even though they are not arts specialist teachers) because it is thought that the arts offer enjoyable post-graduate programmes and assist with general pedagogy.

The Colombian example is an interesting one which documents the connection between teacher education and direct improvements to art education provisions on the ground. *The Law of Culture* (in Colombia) states that "the Ministry of Culture shall provide the conditions required for the professional development of artists and other cultural agents, including art teachers." In light of this, the Ministry of Culture developed the '*Plan Nacional de Música para la Convivencia*', a programme whose main purpose is to train music teachers in different musical practices (chorals, traditional music, wind bands and orchestras). These teachers are trained through university extension courses and workshops. The implementation of the programme in its first year led to the creation of over 700 music schools all over the country. The *Music Conservatory of the National University of Colombia* also developed programmes for music teachers in marginal regions of Colombia, especially in the city of Bogotá. The impact of the teacher education reforms was very evident in the enhanced availability of qualified music teachers and the establishment of a large number of music programmes.

Similarly, between the 1920s and the 1970s, Senegal had arts education integrated into general and technical education and it was then taught by literature, natural science, history and geography, mathematics or even physics and chemistry teachers. However, since the 1970s, the teachers of arts education received subject specific training. Initially that meant arts education was taught by artists, and then by arts education teachers, be it in visual arts or music. The results of this training are evident in the enhanced quality of programmes offered within the schools.

Conversely, in Spain it was noted that there was only limited or no provision for training generalist or specialist teachers. Teachers' salaries are low and the pressures to earn income mean that few teachers attend professional development. This means that arts education is either not taught or poorly taught within the school system. As the respondent from Spain stated, "The great majority of the professors [teachers], struggle to survive with their salary, and very few the teachers try to open new barriers within their profession."

While this section has focused on the benefits of teacher education, especially inservice education, to enhancing the quality of arts education, the research also indicates that partnerships between teachers and artists mediated through professional associations and government and non-government organisations has potential to enhance the quality of teaching pedagogy in general. The following example from Australia suggests that successful policy implementation is dependent upon ongoing support within the school context. It was observed that:

> Sustainable outcomes were achieved in the area of teacher transformation: teacher practice remains flexible with teachers reporting improved quality of relationships with students. However, without ongoing joint planning, team teaching, and in-school mentoring teachers' sense of efficacy is compromised.

Allied to this, the following section outlines some examples of the way issues of teacher disaffection, teacher professionalism and teacher reinvigoration of quality pedagogy have been addressed through arts-rich professional development programmes for teachers.

Arts education's contribution to teacher professional development

- Professional associations and partnerships with artists and arts organisations is an effective model for inservice arts education for teachers.
- Creative partnerships build the pedagogical and critical strengths of all teachers – including those working in non-arts related fields.
- Arts-rich postgraduate programmes are a popular option for teachers and may provide an enticing way to combine arts education inservice with national teacher qualifications and quality frameworks.

Professional development was a significant part of the study, given that earlier questions had revealed that both teachers and artists were directly involved in the implementation of arts programmes but that there was a large variation in the training these professional received and many teachers and artists received no training at all. The level of professional development (inservice education) in the arts varied from no provision to very detailed and systematic provisions. In terms of the latter, New Zealand, Barbados, Singapore, and Nigeria all had specific programmes for the training of teachers to effectively teach the arts in education. For example, in Barbados, the *Ministry* has developed an Arts integrated programme – *Personal Empowerment through the Arts for Creative Education (PEACE Programme)*. Teachers are trained in this programme use the performing arts as a tool for teaching all subject areas.

In many countries, professional associations play a major role in inservice education in the arts. For example, In Singapore the teachers in charge of the drama club were sent for courses with *The Singapore Drama Educators Association* and established theatre companies such as 'Theatreworks'. The respondents from Singapore noted that these courses equipped teachers with the basic skills and knowledge in Speech & Drama to help instil confidence in them, during their deployment as facilitators in class.

A common pattern of professional development was through the formal and informal channels that resulted from involving artists and performance groups directly within the school, working as partners to deliver arts education. For example, in Australia, the involvement of a number of professional artists in schools, such as *Musica Viva* and the *Australian Theatre for Young People* resulted in direct learning for the teachers working collaboratively with the artists to deliver education programmes.

In the Netherlands, UK and USA it was also reported that the long-term partnerships between teachers and artists provided excellent models for professional development. In Austria it was noted that collaboration between artists and teachers led to teachers "thinking and working in new structures and in a new way and opening the school to the public community". It was also noted in Austria, that while the teachers involved in the arts programmes appeared to be more motivated and professionally committed, there was no empirical evidence to suggest a higher level of critical thinking or professional competence. Conversely in Finland, the effect of schools and cultural institutes working together led directly to the development of enhanced teaching methods. It was reported that those teachers who took part in these projects became "very skilful in their teaching". Similarly in Hong Kong it was commented that the experience of teachers designing their lessons with artists and watching or co-teaching with the artist in class resulted in significant professional development for both the artist and the teacher. A particular feature of this programme was the way artists and teachers evaluated together and this gave teachers "some hands-on experience working with the artists" and effectively developed their professional competencies. Key to the effectiveness of partnerships between artists (cultural organisations) and teachers seems to be sustained involvement and shared levels of responsibility and accountability.

Chapter 6:
Goals and indications of quality in arts-rich education

Introduction

Quality arts programmes advantage children's total artistic achievement, but these benefits only accrue where there are valuable provisions. A previous criticism of arts education has been that the goals for arts are too broad, general and all encompassing. Furthermore, even well meaning education and arts organisations have struggled with delineating clear guidelines for the development of quality programmes.

This has gone so far as to say that even ideas of quality cannot be applied to something as esoteric as the arts. By contrast, the international trend to greater monitoring of quality and achievement of goals means that arts education has to be positioned within a framework that allows for evaluative impact measurement. It is also clear, though, that while many of the goals and characteristics of quality arts-rich education and shared with quality education in general, the arts possess a number of particularities.

This chapter explores the role of the arts in provisions of quality education, the characteristics of quality arts education and the goals of arts education. An illuminative example of how quality arts-education often defies boundaries is provided by Het Cultuurnetwerk, in the Netherlands.

> The aim of the project was to evaluate the implementation of the subject *Arts and Cultural Education1* and secondly to find out to what extent it serves its purpose of changing the participation of younger people in the cultural field. *Arts and Education1* is a compulsory subject (introduced in 1998) at the senior school level of general secondary education and pre-university education. In pre-vocational secondary education a somewhat different form of this subject was implemented in 2003. The general goal of *Arts and Cultural Education1* is that students learn to make a motivated choice of cultural activities that are meaningful to them. The core of the subject is the participation in cultural activities such as visiting an exhibition or a concert: so students should experience culture. Most of these cultural visits must be paid for, and to cover part of the expenses the government provides each student with an amount of about 20 euros in vouchers that can be used as payment in museums, theatres, cinemas, etc. Knowledge of arts and culture is not taught by rote learning art historical facts and figures, but by understanding the inter relationships between the different art disciplines by means of a thematic approach. A school is free to choose themes, but there are re-

sources offering teaching models with themes such as 'heroes', 'the city', 'eternal love', etc.

It is also important to note that goals in themselves can be very country or context specific and it is difficult to generalise these beyond borders. It is also apparent that in a number of cases there are stated goals and then more widely applied goals – sometimes in seeming contradiction to the stated goals – that appear in terms of frequently recorded statements, words or concepts embedded in curriculum documentation. For example, in Japan the stated objective include a range of skills and expressive outcomes desired from the programmes of study, but these a complemented by key phrases that appear with frequency throughout the documents including encouraging a love and appreciation of the arts and *"enriching sentiments"*.

Quality Education and Education for All: The role of the arts

- Differences exist between espoused provisions for arts-rich education and the quality received by children
- The impact of arts-rich learning within quality education frameworks tends to be underestimated
- There is insufficient overseeing of the quality of arts programmes

The research indicated that while advocacy to include arts as part of education policy has largely been successful (as stated earlier, as a core part of policy in 84% of countries surveyed), this has not led to wide scale implementation of quality arts programmes at the school level. The current situation sees global monitoring and reporting on educational standards within literacy, mathematics, science and ICT but does not include the impact of arts and cultural experiences within a child's total education. It appears that this is due to an insufficient understanding of the implementation process.

Throughout the results of the survey there is an unequivocal indication that the positive benefits of arts-rich education only occur within the provision of quality programmes. Quality arts education tends to be characterised by a strong partnership between the schools and outside arts and community organisations. In other words it is teachers, artists and the communities, which *together* share the responsibility for the delivery of the programmes.

This research attempted to not simply define arts education and explore its manifestations in practice, but to specifically examine what 'quality' arts education may be. 'Quality' is defined as being those arts education provisions that are of recognised high value and worth in terms of the skills, attitudes and performativity engendered.

Art education focusing on the meaning of gender in the everyday processes of art lessons in school (Finland).

According to Pearsall (1998) quality implies something that has been achieved successfully. In the case of arts education, quality is considered to exist as something that may include achievements (i.e. quality outputs), but goes beyond this to consider learning journeys, pathways, partnerships and recognition. Dewey (1934: 19) writes of quality as being characterised by a "heightened vitality." He further comments that quality signifies, "active and alert commerce with the world: at its height, it implies complete interpretation of self and the world of objects and events." Under this notion, quality is not a fixed disposition but rather as Kissick (1993: 27) notes, "quality is first and foremost an idea, its criteria are susceptible to influences from within a given society."

While global monitoring of educational standards has tended to focus on achievement in mathematics, literacy and scientific thinking, anecdotal comments from children, teachers and parents suggest that the arts have a major impact on schooling and learning. Yet sustained research on the global extent of this impact has been lacking. Concurrently, even if such monitoring of the artistic and cultural aspects of education were to occur, there has not previously existed an agreed set of standards that could be universally established as being evident of quality provisions for art education. The qualities of consummate – or frankly even adequate – arts education have been poorly articulated in the literature.

Yet highly successful arts-rich programmes are apparent in the case studies of everyday practices of arts educators and artists working in a range of educational contexts that form the bulk of this research. It was thus surmised that it may be possible to ascertain the salient qualities that inform principles and practice of effective arts-rich programmes around the world and the impact these successful programmes have. The combination of quantitative and qualitative methods applied in the global research on arts education was premised on the assumption that the elusive qualities apparent in effective arts-rich programmes in a range of contexts may be embedded in case studies of quality practice. Detailed examination of case studies from around the world, given a range of educational, economic and social contexts provided a source of knowledge and enlightenment and shed light on the beliefs, knowledge and practices underpinning arts education. It should be noted that the global research underpinning this book is testament to the diverse nature of the arts. It is certainly not the intention to water down this immensely interesting and varied picture of arts education to fit some simplified model of what a global generic version of arts-rich education might look like. Yet within this multiplicity there are clear patterns in terms of quality provisions and the impact of these worthy programmes. This became the focus of the investigations.

Characteristics of quality arts education

It was a somewhat unexpected result of the research that from all the diversity of case studies presented the parameters of quality were so uniform. From this consistency, it is reasonable to develop a detailed and comprehensive list of the characteristics, in terms of both structure and method that are indicative of – or at least likely to be evident in – quality arts programmes, regardless of the context in which they operate. The following section looks specifically at these characteristics of quality. It is hoped that these might form guidelines by which national systems or individual programmes may be judged to determine their form, merit and worth. High quality education programmes in and through the arts were characterised by:

- Active partnerships between schools and arts organisations and between teachers, artists and the community;
- Shared responsibility for planning, implementation and assessment and evaluation;
- Opportunities for public performance, exhibition and/or presentation;
- A combination of development within the specific art forms (education in the arts) with artistic and creative approaches to learning (education through the arts);

- Provision for critical reflection, problem solving and risk taking;
- Emphasis on collaboration;
- An inclusive stance with accessibility to all children;
- Detailed strategies for assessing and reporting on children's learning, experiences and development;
- Ongoing professional learning for teachers, artists and the community, and
- Flexible school structures and permeable boundaries between schools and the community.

While it could be considered that these pillars of quality are at the heart of all education, a number of case studies indicated that these patterns of qualities were achieved more cost-effectively, more holistically and with greatest 'on the ground' impact within arts-rich educational environments. Substantial studies in the economically developed world – especially Finland, UK, USA, Australia, Canada and Singapore – and in the economically developing world especially Senegal, Nigeria, Barbados and Colombia – suggest that arts-rich curricula have the greatest impact on children' and communities' perceptions of the school, quality learning and teaching and enhanced teacher professionalism.

Quality arts education is the result of interplay of structure and method. This interplay has been explained in Table 10 which exemplifies that way structure and method relate to produce quality outcomes. It should be noted, that these indicators of quality do not specify content. This is deliberate, as the case studies of programmes ranging from small school-based projects to vast national projects show that content is of less relevance to quality than method and structure. Therefore, it is not necessary at an international level to specify content, and in fact it is preferable that this should be derived in relation to local environments, culture and resources. In this way content operates independently of the two major factors impacting on quality provisions. For example, in the Republic of Ireland's project *Artformations* (2005) the shared values which underpinned the programme were a combination of both structural and methodological qualities:

Shared values arising from various collaborations included:
- An art/artist led process
- A child-centred approach
- Holistic development of the child
- Belief that the arts can imaginatively stimulate and also encourage problem solving, affective learning and support social and cultural interactions
- The potential of the arts to help participants to make connections with life and therefore illuminate how we feel and think

Similarly, these indicators of quality hold true for both *education through the arts* and *education in the arts*. In both these complementary ways in which the arts contribute to education, the indicators of quality remain quite stable and consistent.

Table 10: Structural and methodological characteristics of quality arts-rich programmes

Structure	Method
• Active partnership with creative people and organizations • Accessibility to all children • Ongoing professional development • Flexible organizational structures • Shared responsibility for planning and implementation • Permeable boundaries between the school, organization and the community • Detailed assessment and evaluation strategies	• Project-based • Involves teamwork and collaboration • Initiates research • Promotes discussion, exchange of ideas and story telling • Involves formal and informal reflection, that is both formative and summative • Meta critical reflection on learning approaches and changes • Centred around active creation • Is connected and holistic • Includes public performance and exhibition • Utilizes local resources, environment and context for both materials and content • Combines development in the specific languages of the arts with creative approaches to learning • Encourages people to go beyond their perceived scope, to take risks and to use their full potential

The following sections explain in more detail each of these structural and methodological parameters of quality and how they may be implemented in school contexts and at the systemic level. These sections provide an overview of key aspects associated with quality arts provisions, but these indicators need to be read within the context of the broader report that provides more detailed evidence for each of these aspects.

Structural provisions

Active partnership with creative people and organizations

Active partnership involves the direct inclusion of a range of cultural and artistic organizations in all aspects of the planning and delivery of arts education programmes. The most effective programmes have managed to build sustainable, long-term and reciprocal associations with cultural agencies and industries.

These associations need to be authentic partnerships, with all players within the partnership acknowledging the contributions made by the others and being involved in all aspects of decision making, implementation and evaluation. While many schools have had artist-in-residence programmes, these frequently fall short of the level of partnership implied in quality arts provisions. Short-term and tokenistic involvement of creative professionals is unlikely to produce sustained changes in the quality provisions within a school or educational context. Quality partnerships should ideally be for at least two years duration and involve the high level commitment of education, arts and cultural organizations. The Creative Partnerships project in the United Kingdom has instituted a range of partnerships across the education and culture sectors aimed at enhancing arts and educational experiences.

In a number of other countries, including Denmark, France and Japan cultural agencies play an important role in bringing cultural activities into schools. For example, in Japan the *Program for the Promotion of Activities Enabling Children to Experience Culture and Arts"* has been developed to ensure children can experience real art and culture. Yet these sorts of programmes are not partnerships and tend to be more short-term interventions of – and exposure to – cultural agencies rather than sustained partnerships.

Accessibility to all children

Quality programmes are built around the notion of inclusivity and arts-rich education for all. This means that all children, regardless of artistic skills and abilities, initial motivation, behaviour, economic status or other entering attribute, should be entitled to receive high standard arts provisions, both within the various art forms and using creative and artistic approaches to teaching other areas of the curriculum.

This is a particularly important point in relation to initiatives to provide education for all and to look at greater inclusion of a variety of marginalized groups within general education. To meet a baseline in terms of quality arts education, education providers need to ensure that there are arts programmes for ALL children. Providing classes for talented or interested students only cannot be considered as providing a comprehensive education for all. At a practical level, having a school band, choir, dance group, once a year play or art club would not within itself constitute adequate arts education.

Ongoing professional development

The research showed that ongoing professional development had the potential to reinvigorate teachers and creative professionals and to build the confidence, creativity and enjoyment of these groups. The arts helped to re-engage teachers and increased the quality of their overall pedagogy. For artists, working within education was stimulating, inspirational and enhanced their incomes and professional status.

The research indicated that inservice professional development of both creative professionals and teachers was far more effective in improving the quality of arts education than preservice training. At the system level, quality arts education would be characterized by adequate and enduring professional development in the arts and arts-based methods for both teachers and artists. As a cost effective approach, basing artists within educational contexts and supporting sustained partnerships between education and arts organizations seems to be a very efficient way to provide continued professional development. This was particularly the case, where teacher education institutions and universities were part of this partnership process and ongoing professional development could be formally rewarded through enhanced qualifications.

Flexible organizational structures

Quality arts-rich programmes tend to flourish in situations where there is scope for organizational flexibility. Within the education sectors, rigid timetables, compartmentalization of learning and restrictive assessment structures tend to limit the extent and quality of art-rich education.

Similarly, within cultural organizations, high costs, containment within the physical boundaries of a gallery or facility and lack of administrative flexibility limit the likely success of engaging fully with the education sector. Between schools and cultural organizations, there needs to be less rigidity of physical boundaries, such as galleries and performances coming into schools and school days being conducted within cultural facilities and museums. Similarly, schools, museums, theatres and galleries should work more closely with enterprise, industry and higher education sectors. By increasing the permeability between these organizations, it is likely that each will benefit from its blending with the other.

Shared responsibility for planning and implementation

Implied in earlier discussions of both partnerships and flexibility of organization, it is worthy of particular mention that all quality arts-rich programmes included shared responsibility for planning and implementation of all stakeholders.

One of the major inhibitors noted in the research is the widespread lack of consultation between policy makers and those at the coalface of arts education deliver. This results in mismatched aims and inadequate implementation. Similarly, programmes were generally not successful if one or other organization was seen to be both the driving force and leading the implementation. Programmes such as these tended to have short-term success, mainly at the cost of the energy and determination of one or two *champions*, but not generally lead to sustainable programmes over time.

It is crucial therefore, that quality provisions in arts-rich education involve a sharing of responsibility and a democratic approach to planning, policy, implementation and evaluation.

Permeable boundaries between the school, organization and the community

While this point has already been canvassed to some extent in terms of flexibility of organizational structures, there is need to draw specific attention to the value of the inclusion of community within the development of quality arts education programmes.

Both schools and arts and cultural organizations need to be prepared to open their boundaries – both actual and metaphoric – to the influences of the community within which they exist. This is particularly the case within marginalized communities where the perceptions of both schools and cultural organizations tend to be one that is quite negative and often based on misconceptions, generalizations and senses of alienation.

The histories of both schools and cultural organizations have not been conducive to open and democratic participation of minority groups within communities. To redress this, affirmative action does need to be undertaken to reach out to these groups. Exhibition and performance afford wonderful opportunities to more fully engage the community in education and cultural provisions and can act as a catalyst enabling greater community participation.

Detailed assessment and evaluation strategies

One of the most significant and widespread findings from the research case studies is that there is an urgent need for methods of assessment that more fully recognize the contribution of arts and cultural components within children's education. While over half the countries surveyed assessed the arts, the case studies indicated that methods of assessment for creative learning were poorly developed and lacked recognition within the formal assessment processes. This means that arts learning is frequently poorly documented and lacks substantiation and status within educational processes.

Concurrently, inappropriate assessment strategies were seen to have a direct inhibiting impact on quality programmes. Over reliance on outcomes-based assessment, assessment of only a limited number of education disciplines and dominant external examination were seen as factors hindering quality arts education. Allied to this, impact evaluation in the arts is similarly inadequate. As many arts-rich programmes operate on limited funding, financial provision is rarely made to adequately evaluate and report the results of the programme. The arts within education have been characterized by numerous instances of wonderful programmes, but almost no substantial evaluation of these programmes.

In several countries, namely England, Canada, Finland, and to a lesser extent India, Singapore, Australia and New Zealand, systematic procedures have been put in place to evaluate and document the impact of arts-rich education. Where these systems exist, there appears to be a flow-on effect to improvements in the quality of programmes, driven by the enhanced perceptions within the schools that the arts are a valued part of a child's total education.

While almost every country gives lip service to the value of the arts in education, it is those countries which back this policy rhetoric with sound evaluation and monitoring strategies who witness the greatest improvement in overall quality at the school and classroom level. The value of evaluation in leading quality improvement was clearly indicated in a number of countries. As was noted in the Republic of Ireland's *Poetry Ireland: Writers in Schools Schemes*, "evaluation is a crucial element in programme implementation and a key tool in planning and policy development."

Combined with these structural aspects most commonly found in high quality programmes, there are a number of methodological elements that seem to be manifest in high quality arts-rich education.

Project-based

The most significant aspect of methodology that appeared in the qualitative case studies of effective arts-based education was the arousal of children's curiosity about the world through problem or project orientated activities. In diverse case studies, respondents felt that an open, imaginative and creative mind was a vital aspect of all learning, and most fully developed through engagement with project-based arts activities.

Effective project-based arts-rich education involved the child in investigations of their direct environment and responding to issues around them through their art making process. For example, in Malaysia the concepts of access, equity and quality were evident in the project-based *Anak Anak Kota* (Children of the City) programme. This allowed the young people involved to explore their cultural and historical identities through creative arts initiatives conducted within the inner city environments of the children. The children not only engaged in the activities presented, but actively designed the scope and nature of the underpinning projects.

Initiates research

A key characteristic possessed within all the quality case studies was the teacher's ability to be flexible and adaptable in their teaching and to provide tasks that initiated research inquiry amongst the children. A research-orientated approach combines with project-based methods to encourage an educational climate where the teachers, artists and children are encouraged to engage in learning conversations and to test their ideas, adjusting rapidly to spontaneous situations to create interesting and meaningful art-based learning opportunities.

Quality arts-based programmes adopted experimental models of teaching. Artists, teachers and children engaged in such programmes tried things and tested ideas in an initiatory way. They reflected on these experiments, adapting the content accordingly. This adventurous approach may initially appear spontaneous and unplanned, but more correctly represented an inquiry method of learning, based on flexibility of choices governed by sound evaluation practices.

Effective programmes as presented in the case studies were ready to abandon preconceived plans and move with the spontaneous arts learning opportunities. For example, a number of projects being undertaken in Hong Kong as part of the *One Child Foundation* scheme take an innovative and adventurous approach to young people's education. Activities such as *Creative Campus TV* allowed children to take a higher level of control within the education process and use the arts as a language of empowerment.

Centred around active creation

All of the quality programmes placed major value on active arts making and performance and exhibition. It was asserted that engagement in arts creation engendered particular learning and achievement, only possible when embedded within active practice. Of particular importance was that children received opportunities to create in a broad range of the arts. In many case studies, creative experiences may only involve one or two of the arts (especially music and visual arts). Many children did not receive sustained opportunities to actively engage in dance or drama to see local or heritage art forms practiced within the school day.

While active creation was a feature of most early years' programmes, the extent of this involvement could be quite limited. For example, in Fiji, a child might only get 1 art period out of a 40-period week. Many countries reported only sporadic arts provisions. The arts were often electives within the later years, meaning some children may never get to engage in active creation of the arts.

At other times, active engagement was limited by inadequate human and fiscal resources that meant not every child had the opportunity to get 'hands on' opportunities. In some countries, overcrowded classrooms prevented active creation opportunities.

Conversely, children repeatedly noted the value of participating in performances and exhibitions. This was particularly beneficial when mediated by an artist.

Is connected and holistic

The case studies of quality practice underpinned the importance of connecting learning experiences in the arts into meaningful sequences and clusters. By contrast, poor quality arts experiences were described as being those programmes that were tokenistic, isolated and disconnected – from children, their environment and other learning. Connected arts programmes were premised on the arts' capacity for building better relationship with the children. To enable connected learning to be most effective, time (and timetables) had to be more flexible and the arts-based aspects of learning needed to relate to other aspects of the children's learning such as language learning, literature, story writing and history studies.

While there was overwhelming support for the involvement of artists in educational settings, the artists had to be perceived as total partners in the educational endeavour and not as 'specialists' existing outside the general educational processes. It was considered that specialists were hampered in their ability to develop arts-based lessons that could be fully integrated with other subjects.

Involves teamwork and collaboration

A key feature of quality arts-based programmes appears to be the way they assist in the development of group work and team collaborations in a non-competitive manner. The collaborative nature of creative arts-based projects – especially those within dance and drama – were seen to actively encourage collaborative working on different stages or aspects of a project.

Quality arts-based projects tended to extend over for several weeks – or more – and children worked at their own pace within the collaborative project framework. Additionally, some programmes encouraged the children to work on a number of projects both concurrently and over time.

Promotes discussion, exchange of ideas and story telling

Quality arts-based programmes involved an active sharing of ideas and conversations between artists, teachers and children. In particular, they placed importance on children's feelings and the manner in which the arts allowed for expression of individuality. High quality programmes provide a range of enticing and varied learning experiences aimed at encouraging the child to unfold their ideas.

Under this conception the child is acknowledged as an artist, and while the teachers and artists provided levels of formal instruction, this was intended to nurture ideas and skills and stimulate aesthetic conversations rather than provide closed directions. All children were perceived to possess the potential for artistic expression and so the emphasis was on studio production and performance underpinned by encouraging conceptual development through making, verbal and at times with older students, written, conversations within the group of children and between the teacher and the children.

Involves formal and informal reflection, that is both formative and summative

Formal and informal contemplative practices were valued as a way to encourage the children to view their work more critically and reflectively. Processes of journal writing and visual and verbal journals were common in several of the case studies. In other instances, reflective processes were less formalised and would use conversations, images and actions to instigate and maintain the reflective processes.

In some innovative examples, children had developed detailed research and documentation skills to record their learning and reflect on this learning process. In the *Chicago Arts Partnerships in Education (CAPE),* for example, the young people used digital photography to record and reflect on their learning and the children were encouraged to be active researchers in the learning process.

Meta critical reflection on learning approaches and changes

Similar to the children being encouraged to build reflective practices, both educators and artists engaged in formative and summative reflective practices. It appeared in the case studies that there existed certain strategies and combinations of behaviours that were consistently held across the variety of case studies and appeared to be successful in a range of contexts. While these are generally embedded in the way the programme operates, it was evident that quality arts-rich education – and the teachers and artists within them – possess a set of ideas, theories and practices that were continually assessed to determine the application and interplay of these in different situations and in response to pluralistic contexts.

In this way, these beliefs and practices formed a set accomplished ideals that, as Smith (1993) describes, make sense to us, not absolutely in all times and places but in our own time and place. In this way, ideals of accomplished practice in arts education might be quite transient. As May (1993: 55) contends: "I couldn't assume that what I did would be feasible or right for anyone else." Good learning and teaching are inevitably context dependent.

Dahllof (1991: 112) argues that, in a given situation, certain strategies and combinations of behaviours and beliefs may be more effective than others, but that these will be impacted upon by the nature and interest of the students, the phase of the learning cycle, the subject matter, and specific goals. The teachers and artists made direct links between the children's environment and their art learning, while at the same time presenting provocations and problems that challenged the children to move from their immediate environment and question previously held beliefs and ideals.

Includes public performance and exhibition

The positive benefits of performance and exhibition were evident in the outcomes of quality arts-rich education. From one perspective, it was considered that a performance outcome provide effective ways to engender a positive school profile, build community links and to showcase the work of the children. It was also suggested that the arts are a performance or exhibition based medium and as such the presentation of the work remains an important aspect of the programme. Performance and exhibitions generated publicity for arts-based education and allowed the work of the teachers, artists and children to be more publicly highlighted. This was of particular benefit in raising the confidence and self-esteem of the children involved and by promoting more favourable views of the school and its local community.

Conversely, there was some concern that performance and exhibition outcome might adversely impact on the goals of a project and that the creative process might be compromised by having to work to a performance outcome and that this in turn would mean that the performance might 'drive' learning rather than the performance or exhibition emerging out of learning.

To this extent, the creative process, risk-taking and experimentation were more important than achieving an attractive end product. Furthermore, an over-reliance on producing a high quality end product may be detrimental to the children engaging in exploratory and risk-orientated processes.

Despite these caveats, all the case studies referred to the significance of audience in the artistic process. Exhibition and performance exist as a way to bring kudos to the children and their arts experiences and as a tool to promote the benefits of arts-rich education to a wider audience. Several case studies also pointed to the manner in which performance and exhibition give children 'voice' and can be powerful advocacy tools for promoting the value of arts education.

Utilizes local resources, environment and context for both materials and content

Quality programmes allowed children to make artistic connections within their local environment. Through the use of local artists and artworks, the teachers hope that the children will make personal connections with art. The qualitative comments suggest that the arts have strong powers of social change and can be used it to build the children's self-esteem and address social justice and equity issues within the community. To this extent, the use of local resources within arts-rich education enables children's needs to be addressed more appropriately.

In Brazil for example, arts education projects were dealing with environmental issues; while in Korea issues of land use featured; in Australia questions of gender equity and in Bhutan religious beliefs were at the core of artistic practices. In effective arts-rich education, the content frequently dealt with issues of local importance especially heritage, health or environmental themes.

Local resources were also at the hub of quality arts-rich education. Use of local instruments in music education; locally available materials for art making; time honoured traditions for dances and role playing on the stages of the children's lives were at the heart of quality programmes. For example in Bhutan, the readily available bamboo was used as the basis of art making. In Senegal, hair became the resource for exploration of patterns through braiding. Contemporary stories about youth alienation were retold through shadow puppets and effective drama and dance programmes were undertaken in the space next to the classrooms in Cambodia. Quality teachers make ingenious use of local contexts and resources to develop effective programmes of instruction and induction into the skills and values of the arts.

On a cautionary note, several of the non-western countries had in recent years adopted – somewhat uncritically – models of western education, including western models of arts education. This had led to archetypes of arts education more closely aligned with European fine arts and music and less connected with the rich cultural traditions of their own countries. The formalisation of the education processes in many countries has undermined local artistic heritage and devalued the inclusion of more local community practices in the arts.

Combines development in the specific languages of the arts with creative approaches to learning

The development of language skills appeared to be central within the design and implementation of arts-rich education. This idea was enacted in two ways. Firstly, language was seen to have an important function to perform in giving student the words and language to enable children to talk about their artwork, performance and the work of artists. They encouraged the children to talk to each other about their arts experiences.

Image courtesy of
Operation Art (Australia)

The second view of the value of the arts as language was linked to the expression of feeling. The arts were seen as a powerful form of communication. It was also felt that children possess many languages of learning and that these are rarely excited within traditional education.

Encourages people to go beyond their perceived scope, to take risks and to use their full potential

Quality arts-rich education encouraged the children to take risks and allowed them to make mistakes. 'Letting go' of control and being confident to enable children make mistakes was important part of giving children ownership of their creative processes. Uncertainty surrounds quality arts practice and this is to be encouraged.

Quality arts education programmes have impact on the child; the teaching and learning environment, and; on the community, but these benefits were only observed where quality programmes were in place. Poor quality and inadequate programmes do little to enhance the educational potential of the child or build first-rate schools. It is of significance to note that a number of case studies indicated that bad and poor quality programmes, in fact may be detrimental to children's creative development and adversely effect teacher confidence and the participation of cultural agencies.

Given that, it is important that the rhetoric of policy that supports the inclusion of arts education within the total educational experiences of the child is backed by substantial implementation and monitoring structures that ensures children receive high quality programmes. These programmes are no more expensive to implement than poor quality programmes and afford the opportunity to initiate sustained educational reform and greatly enhance the overall excellence of education. The argument should be less about *Education for All* and more about quality learning provisions for all. In this regard, the arts have an enormous amount to offer education.

The following chapter explores the impact of arts-rich education. The impacts documented are predicated on the assumption that these impacts result from quality programmes that to a large extent are characteristic of the methods and contents that have been described and analysed in this chapter.

Chapter 7:
The impact of arts education

Introduction

This chapter summarises the main impacts of arts education and documents the benefits of an arts-rich curriculum as revealed through the quantitative and qualitative data in the survey.

The goals of arts education

- Cultural, social and aesthetic goals are the main reasons given for arts education.
- Goals of art education programmes vary within formal and informal education settings.

Cultural (88%), social (84%) and aesthetic (84%) goals were seen by the responding countries as being the main goals of art education. Allied to this, personal goals (64%) were also seen to be of value. Less value was placed on literacy goals (56%), while economic (44%) and numeracy goals (44%) were of least importance (see Table 10 on page 114).

The other goal identified in qualitative comments was the goal assigned to the arts of building nationhood. The Republic of the Seychelles suggested that political goals underpin arts education, especially in the way that arts education builds ideas of nationhood. This comment was also echoed in the Netherlands where it was suggested that a goal of art education was the development of democratic competencies and building greater equity in cultural participation. In Senegal, it was noted that art education may have therapeutic goals aligned to the physical and mental well being of the children.

Several countries indicated that the goals assigned to arts education varied within the different contexts in which the art education occurred. For example, artistic and aesthetic goals tended to be more the focus of outside of school hours programmes, while programmes within schools may centre more on cultural and social goals. To be able to extrapolate further from this data, it would be useful to gather more information on how each country interpreted the content of these key goals. For example, it could be implied that cultural goals are more aligned to building sustainable communities, whereas social goals may be more associated with building a sustainable individual or classroom environment. In many countries, reference to cultural goals was very closely aligned with the protection and promotion of artistic heritage and the preservation of culturally specific arts practices. It would also be interesting to pursue in more detail the perceived impact of such goals on the general education potential of the child and their learning in and through the arts.

Whatever the goals of arts education, these goals are only achieved where quality programmes exist. Despite the cultural and contextual differences – and it could also be argued research methodological differences – there were clear and unequivocal indicators of quality that existed regardless of the goals, scope or context of programmes.

There was significant and consistent evidence that arts-rich education contributed to improved children's achievement both within the arts and more generally across education. The caveat of that finding was that this only seemed to be the case in examples of effective practice and quality educational provisions. In comparative case studies, educational settings that contained quality provisions of arts-rich pedagogy consistently outperformed their more traditional (arts-lacking) counterparts.

It is important to note in interpreting the statistical evidence in this and subsequent sections that there was considerable variation in numerical evidence related to documented benefits. This variation can be explained in terms of significant out-lying cases. To understand this variation in statistical data it was imperative to interpret these in terms of the substantial qualitative comments made. When this analysis was undertaken, what became clear was that, when talking of benefits, the discussion needs to be limited to effective examples, whereas poor arts education appears to have no – or a negative – effect on children's learning. This underlines the importance of providing high quality programmes. For example, while 70% of respondents acknowledged the contribution of arts education to children's artistic achievement, 20% of respondents suggested that arts education had either no benefit or a negative impact. When this is interpreted in conjunction with the qualitative comments, it is apparent that benefit only accrues where quality exists.

Arts-rich education improves achievement in the arts

- Arts-rich education improves skills and competencies within the arts
- Specific programmes are beneficial for the children involved but may not be more broadly applied to general education

In the USA very effective arts-rich education programmes led to dramatic increases in students' achievement in the arts, but there is also an implication that these programmes are isolated examples that the broader education situation, as the following comment indicates:

Specific projects (*CAPE* in Chicago, *The Village of Art and Humanities* in Philadelphia, *Young Playwrights Festivals* throughout the US, *The Digital Playground* at the *Hoboken Charter School, Intermedia Arts* in Minneapolis, *Studio Museum* in Harlem, *Young Chicago Authors* in Chicago, *Free Street Theatre* in Chicago, the *East Bay Center for the Performing Arts* in Richmond California, the *Armoury Center for the Arts* in Pasadena California, *Jump-Start Performance Company* in San Antonio, Texas, etc.) have demonstrated radical increases in student achievement in the arts.

This pattern of specific positive programmes seems to be the case in most countries. Highly successful examples of arts-rich education have clearly documented benefits, but despite this, these good programmes may operate as relatively isolated examples within the broader national picture as this analysis from Colombia suggests:

Although there are not many private or public projects supporting student artistic achievement, there are some remarkable efforts such as: *Colegio del Cuerpo, Batuta, Incolballet, Tejedores de Sociedad, Circo para todos, Plan Nacional de Música para la Convivencia, Sistema de Escuelas de Arte del Norte de Santander, Programa de Orquestas Sinfónicas Juveniles e Infantiles "Batuta", Música en los Templos*, among others.

A similar position was noted in China where it was observed that specific projects like the musical, *Cantonese and Beijing Opera, Shadow Puppet Show* "provide ample opportunities for the students to experience the arts under the artists' expertise." Yet these programmes tend to operate outside the parameters of formal education and engage comparatively few students.

Successful programmes tend to be of most benefit to arts learning if there is provision for children to exhibit their arts learning in some form of public performance, presentation or forum. For example in Canada there are, "arts shows and theatre performances that tour the country, all based in work done in arts programmes in schools."

In Germany, the "results [of the art education programmes] and artistic improvement can be seen in school-concerts and school-representations. All forms of after-school cultural and arts education of artists, cultural institutions and organizations have many forms of artistic presentations and contributions to the cultural life of the community." These presentations were not only viewed as a positive experience for children and their parents, but also as a way to showcase and document the children's learning in the arts.

Several of the responding countries indicated that there was insufficient empirical data related to the benefits of sustained art education on children's cultural and artistic achievements and that more research was required to ascertain impact, especially in terms of longitudinal changes. There was also a lack of research evidence that isolated specific aspects of arts-rich learning to key types of learning within any one or more of the art forms. More research is required to analyse the general benefits noted and to interpret the manner in which certain characteristics of arts-rich education may directly or indirectly lead to specified arts outcomes. Conversely, it could be argued that the arts are holistic in nature and the more generalised benefits noted may be best understood in terms of generic skills rather than discreet learning areas. This area of research should be prioritised in the future.

While the previously referred to examples are more isolated examples of the positive impact of arts education, in several countries widespread approaches have shown substantial benefits in enhanced artistic and cultural understanding. For example, in Finland several national studies have been conducted that show artistic, health and educational benefits. These very detailed national studies conducted over a number of years consistently show positive benefits.

> We have some surveys about the topic: 1. *Schools and cultural institutes working together* (project took place 1998-2001) (NBE) 2. *Cultural heritage programme, the Oak of Finland,* (1999-2004) (NBE). Both of these programmes gave the positive results. 3. *Health and artistic activities* (children) (Stakes).

In Senegal, it was noted that the artistic benefits generated by effective arts education were not only to the individuals involved (such as career opportunities) but extended more broadly into the community (such as the transferral of values and in community achievement across a range of disciplines). The Senegalese research indicated three distinct benefits that accrued from arts education:

> 1) Former pupils in arts education from secondary schools have chosen to carry on in higher education with artistic professions or arts education. Today, they are among our specialists;
> 2) Apart from the official curriculum, arts education in the communities is a way to maintain the passing on of the knowledge and know-how in traditional disciplines;
> 3) International, national and local arts and cultural events show the creations of artists or arts education classes and usually have an impact on the public – be it from schools or universities – and favour future applications for studies in arts, literature, philosophy and sciences.

Conversely, a number of countries identified that a lack of arts education had been detrimental to the child's total development especially in the enhancement of creativity. In the following example from the Republic of Seychelles it was noted that, while some limited arts education (skills-based) had been introduced in this country – and had resulted in some noted improvements in aspects such as motor skills – the more widespread benefits of the arts had not occurred because of the limiting structure of the programme:

> With the exception of rote drawing, painting and craftwork endeavours, no arts education projects as defined in the survey have been initiated at school level. Curiosity and creativity are not viewed as positive life skills, particularly at primary level. However, general consensus admits that students' motor and technical skills (but NOT creativity) have dramatically improved over the last 10 years.

While this section has focused on the benefits to arts learning that occurs as the result of quality arts programmes, effective arts-rich education was also seen to have more general benefits to improved educational achievement.

Arts education's contribution to improved student educational attainment and academic achievement

- Quality arts education programmes lead to improvements in academic achievement
- Literacy is significantly enhanced through arts education
- Arts-rich education enhances performance in language learning
- Arts education leads to an improvement in student, parental and community perceptions of schools

Art has an intrinsic value but the view that art is of value in itself does not preclude additional educational benefits. One of the main findings evident in the responses from every country is that quality arts-rich programmes have positive effects on educational attainment.

The data indicated that 71% of quality arts programmes had led to direct improvements in academic achievement. In a number of instances there was strong national or case study empirical data to support the proposition that arts education programmes improve students' academic attainment. For example, in a study conducted in the USA found:

Learning in and with the arts has been linked with increased student achievement, but the means by which the arts may support cognitive growth in students is relatively undocumented. Thirty students across ten classes in veteran teacher/artist partnerships were selected to explore the processes and outcomes associated with arts-integrated learning units versus learning processes and outcomes in comparable non-arts units. The student sample evenly represented comparatively high, medium, and low achievers. Even though we observed differences in levels of arts integration across classrooms, students from all achievement levels displayed significant increases in their ability to analytically assess their own learning following arts-integrated units. No such gains were associated with traditional instructional experiences. Students also described their arts-integrated versus non-arts learning differently. Arts-integrated instruction: 1) created more independent and intrinsically motivated investments in learning, 2) fostered learning for understanding as opposed to recall of facts for tests, 3) transformed students' characterizations of "learning barriers" into "challenges" to be solved, and 4) inspired students to pursue further learning opportunities outside of class.

In a very substantial Singaporean national study it was found that, while significant improvements were noted in arts education development, engagement in the arts had led directly to enhanced literacy and English language performance. The study conducted over three years demonstrated that:

- There was an improvement of 'O' level Art results, from 50% passes in 2002 to 100% pass with 33% distinctions in 2003.
- From teachers' and parents' feedback, students displayed an increase in level of confidence in their usage and expression of English language after the *Speech & Drama* programme was implemented.

Of those countries submitting observed statistical research data on student achievement, the improvements noted bore remarkable similarities across quite diverse case studies. In terms of literacy, the improvement noted ranged between 18-24% with an average of 22% improvement. In mathematics, the range of reported improvements was between a 3% and 15% improvement noted in different studies, with an average reported improvement of 6%. As only a few countries had substantially measured improvement in language results (learning of languages other than the mother tongue or home language of the child) it is not possible to provide large-scale statistical evidence, yet those cases that had measured this aspect of arts-rich learning reported significant improvements (see the detailed example from Singapore that follows p. 109). This particular aspect of impact research warrants further investigation.

In Canada a number of detailed and comprehensive longitudinal studies have repeatedly indicated the connection between engagement in quality arts programmes and improved student achievement. Interestingly, these studies also highlighted a reduced dropout rate and enhanced student cooperation and positive school learning environment.

> The *Learning Through the Arts (LTTA)* 3-year evaluation *National Arts and Youth Demonstration Project (NAYDP)* [demonstrated that] students enrolled in the LTTA programme have shown improvement across most if not all subject (i.e. non-arts classes as well) LTTA has seen significant increases in standardized test scores over non-LTTA schools. Participants in the NAYDP have shown improvements scholastically; that they have a lower drop out rate; and a higher level of educational achievement.

Furthermore, the *Learning Through the Arts (LTTA)* project established in 1995 by the *Royal Conservatory of Music* and has become a national leader in preschool and education music programmes. The project combines artists and teachers with the aim of expanding learning opportunities fro young people. It involves an approach to learning through the arts, where the arts are used to access concepts and make meaning. The project involves over 100,000 students, in 240 schools in six Canadian cities. Using interviews, case studies, focus groups and photographs, the project had major impact nationally and involved the cooperation of universities, arts organisations, schools and the community. The findings indicate that children involved in the project were: more likely to read for pleasure; spend less time watching TV and playing video games; as well as they perform better on language and mathematics tests. While such impressive findings are always open to methodological debates, the results are very significant indeed.

These results were mirrored in a number of other countries. In Australia, the *Education and Arts Partnership Initiative (EAPI)* research had shown strong causal links between the inclusion of arts education and improved academic and social outcomes from school, particularly in the area of literacy. A comprehensive study across a number of cases in Australia funded by the Australian Government through the *Department of Education, Science and Training,* the Australia Council and the *Department of Communications, Information Technology and the Arts* provides further evidence that exposure to the arts provides positive general learning outcomes, particularly for young people who are Indigenous, in remote or regional communities or from disadvantaged backgrounds. The selected sites offered a variety of arts programmes with a focus on drama (at two sites, *Youth Arts with an Edge* and *Arts@Direk*) and music (at two sites in the Northern Territory, *Boys' Business* and the *Indigenous Music Education Programme*). There was a range of ages from Year 4 (primary) to Year 10 (secondary) and a diverse range of backgrounds amongst the participating students. The diversity of sites necessitated a variety of evaluation strategies. The outcomes from the study substantiate evidence that involvement in arts programmes has a positive impact on students' engagement with learning and, for students from Indigenous communities, leads to improved attendance at school (attendance was not seen as an issue at other schools). For example, in one case, a Year 4 'arts-rich' group scored significantly higher than a matched 'non-arts-rich' group on the generic competencies of problem solving, planning and organising, communication and working with others.

Similarly, the *'Bastian-study'* in Germany proves that music-education in schools contributes to improved levels of educational attainment. Empirical work in the USA correlates the presence of quality arts programmes with improvements in educational attainment. These include *CAPE* in Chicago, *Big Thought* (Young Audiences of North Texas) in Dallas, the *A+ Schools* in North Carolina, the *New England Conservatory Charter School* in Boston, and the large number of studies identified in the *Champions of Change* document.

In Australia, a project evaluating the impact of a music programme upon the educational outcomes of Indigenous learners according to recognised numeracy and English literacy benchmarks and community expectations, as contained in the *National Indigenous English Literacy and Numeracy Strategy (NIELNS)* found that arts education "allowed students to experience academic achievement and access employment options by the pathway most valued by mainstream Australian society; that is through standard Australian English literacy and numeracy outcomes."

This educational improvement was particularly evidenced in areas such as literacy learning, language learning and individual and social development of the child. An extensive study investigating the impact of drama strategies on the development of oral language proficiency at *Secondary 4 level (Normal Technical Stream)* conducted in Singapore found that the use of artistic pedagogy had a marked impact on children's assessment scores in English language learning as the following details of their research shows:

The project is a design experiment that tests whether the use of drama as a learning process produces better or different results for students in their *Sec Four Normal Technical* oral results.

The participants are students in their tenth year of schooling, about 16 years of age, in the lowest school stream (comparable to *D stream*). Four schools participated. Each school nominated a class of 40 for intervention and two of the schools nominated another class, of the same level as schooling, as controls. The four intervention groups were taken by *test facilitators* while the two control groups carried on with usual lessons with their English Language teachers. None of the students from all six classes had prior drama lessons.

The research involved 10 lessons, each lasting an hour. These were planned and implemented as either two lessons per week for 5 weeks or one lesson per week for 10 weeks. Instead of drama games and exercise which promotes oral communication, the format was in contextualized activities within four drama pieces. Students had to work in and out of role, in small and large groups and collaborated to solve tasks that were set. Language activities included interviewing, collaborative creating roles and relationships, explaining, describing, questioning, etc.

Data was collected via facilitators' journals and interviews with facilitators, regular English teachers and randomly selected students. Pre-test and post-tests were also conducted with randomly selected students. The tests emulated very closely the *GCE 'N' level Oral* examination. The examiners were teachers whom students were unfamiliar with. The tests involved conversation questions with picture stimulus. Examiners would ask preliminary, descriptive, and interpretive questions to orientate the students to the themes in the picture. Questions were open-ended, addressing issues of personal opinion, experience, and so on.

Oral test results from the *Intervention* groups and *Control* groups were analysed and compared. The following conclusions were made:
- The results for pre-tests, for both intervention and control groups, had similar scores.
- The results for post tests indicated that the intervention group performed consistently better.
- The intervention group showed improvement on ALL assessment measures, not just in one particular area.

Interviews with students cited that there was an improvement in self-confidence, awareness that they can speak more fluently and a break down of barriers across ethnic groups.

Furthermore, schools that contained arts-rich curricula were more likely to be viewed as positive and effective places by the children, their parents and the broader community.

Carlos Mario Lema. Colombia, Plan Nacional Música para la convivencia. Photo courtesy of Monica Romero and Clarisa Ruiz.

There was also sustained evidence that arts-rich environments can enhance general community sustainability, especially in 'at risk' community settings. In Canada, the *National Arts and Youth Demonstration Project (NAYDP)*, a three-year demonstration study, initiated in 2001 and implemented in five sites across Canada, in which the aim was to explore art programmes as an alternative pathway to enhancing the life chances of children and youth in lower income communities in the country found that:

> [The] project has had a very positive regenerative impact at the local level, extending from student to family to community. Within the children it has been observed that there is increased confidence, pride, self awareness, interest in the arts, respect for others, and engagement in the community. Parents and the community interviewed also reported similar changes. For the artists who were partners in this project, their participation acted as a catalyst, expanding and infusing their existing arts practices, developing additional skills and making stronger connection to their community.

In addition to these empirical studies, many respondents pointed to specific anecdotal evidence of enhanced educational achievement. For example, New Zealand, improvements in academic attainment were reported by parents and teachers.

Related to the issue of academic attainment, a number of countries referred to the anecdotal evidence that the 'climate' of the school had improved significantly because of the inclusion of arts education and this had indirectly led to improved student attainment. These skills were often seen as generic learning skills that were directly transferable to improved academic results. A number of comments were made similar to this one from the Netherlands:

> Arts education stimulates children to give the best they can, they develop their talents in a secure environment and they are challenged in an appropriate way. That gives them self-confidence and courage to face new situations. Their communication skills are very good and they are curious for new 'knowledge'.

Of particular relevance, was the manner in which a number of countries identified that the development of problem solving, critical thinking and collaborative skills directly attributed to arts education and had positive effects on academic attainment. For example, Austria noted that the social component of working in a process-orientated basis and in groups – as occurs in quality arts education – influences and improves the level of educational realization. The respondents from China noted that "projects of learning through the arts managed to develop students' generic skills in general" and this led to "enhanced student academic achievement" (see Tables 9 and 10).

Table 9: Perceived contribution of arts education to improved
levels of educational attainment (%)

Agree	38
Strongly Agree	33
Don't Know	21
Disagree	8
Strongly Disagree	0
No answer/invalid/illegible	11
Please give examples (insert text)	0
Total	100

Cumulative percentages

Table 10: Contribution of arts education to general education goals

Cultural goals	88
Social goals	84
Artistic/aesthetic goals	84
Personal goals Economic goals	64
Literacy goals	56
Numeracy goals	44
Economic goals	44
Other (insert text)	0
No answer/invalid/illegible	7

The respondents were permitted to indicate multiple responses
hence the percentages are not cumulative.

Several countries identified a correlation between the inclusion of arts within the curriculum and an improvement in student, parental and community perceptions of schools. While not empirically linked to improved academic outcomes, improved community attitudes to the school, as generated through the arts, had a bearing on academic achievement. For example, in Austria, all the schools that received the highest ratings in terms of public appreciation are providing more cultural activities than their counterpart schools. The positive benefits of arts education to general school achievement and community perceptions of schools were evident in the results from Senegal that stated that:

Arts education is in constant interaction with the other academic subjects:
- Philosophy and aesthetics;
- Mathematics;
- Languages and literature through arts and culture;
- Graphs in natural science, history and geography;
- Physical education;
- Decorating the school or university premises;
- Organising leisure activities; and,
- Organising parties and ceremonies.

Moreover, many country leaders – in fields as different as Public Services, Justice, Army, Sports, Politics, Business, etc. – like to underline the links between their present or past artistic activities and their working and decision-making capacities (organization, adaptability, elocution, diction, relaxation, leisure, etc.)

Once again, the call was made for greater empirical research to document the benefits, or otherwise of arts education to student achievement. This was supported by the quantitative data that indicated in approximately one quarter of all countries there was insufficient evidence to ascertain the impact of the arts on educational achievement. It was also noted that in 8% of cases, arts education is either non-existent or of such low quality that there are no benefits possible. As the Republic of Seychelles noted, it is impossible to have any educational benefits if arts education is non-existent in the country. This was also the case in Spain, where there was concern that the reduction in arts education and the converse increase in digital and television exposure were adversely effecting learning and cultural education.

Arts education's contribution to improved student attitude

- Arts-rich programmes improve students' attitudes to school.
- Arts education increases co-operation, respect, responsibility, tolerance, and appreciation.
- Arts education has a positive impact on the development of social and cultural understanding.
- More longitudinal research is needed on the impact of arts education.

The figures related to the contribution of arts education to improved student attitude (71% of countries agreed or strongly agreed that a rich-arts education programme improved students' attitude to school) were similar to those noted for improved learning. It could be assumed that a correlation may exist between improved student attitude and improvements in arts and academic outcomes. Once again, the qualitative comments also highlighted the imperative for quality programmes. The relatively high (20%) of "don't know" answers also points to the need for more sustained research on the impact of arts education. This appears to be particularly the case in relation to the need for more substantial evaluation studies to determine specific pedagogical and learning indicators of quality implementation and the longitudinal impact of this implementation on the child and their attitude and learning.

Canada, Australia, the UK, the USA and Finland all have detailed studies that indicate that quality arts education leads to enhanced student attitudes and confidence. Within a number of other countries there was strong anecdotal evidence to suggest that involvement in the arts makes a major contribution to a child's emotional well being, confidence and attitude to school.

In Nigeria it was acknowledged that arts education improved children's skills and attitude to life. This view was echoed from the Austrian observations that suggested that the arts led to "different points of view [and] help to open the mind." Similarly in China there was the view that arts education made children "enjoy learning more in general [and] have more self confidence in themselves and have improved communication with their peers." In Australia, involvement in arts programmes had led to improved engagement and attendance at school for indigenous students. Senegal noted that pupils in arts education classes are able to: "work in group; show generosity, intellectual curiosity, imagination, humour; express constructive appreciation; accept observations on their work; and understand the meaning of competition."

Canada had a very detailed programme for evaluating the social and attitudinal benefit of the arts. It was reported in Canada, that "for 'social issues' in schools, the arts are routinely the first response made by school boards and principals." Research accompanying the Canadian projects supports the way the arts contribute to improved student attitude and confidence. Details of these can be found in the *National Arts and Youth Demonstration* project and the *Arts Network for Children and Youth (ANCY)*. The first is a research project which goes into communities of high risk youth, parents and teachers and documents improved behaviour as a result arts education. ANCY is an association of programmes and organizations, many of which partner with organizations and government departments and agencies (Heath and Welfare, Justice, Royal Canadian Mounted Police, local authorities, community and recreation centres).

The Canadian respondents also underlined the value of building arts education experiences beyond the traditional school boundaries as a way of influencing attitudes and building student confidence. Studies conducted in Canada suggest that partnerships with non-government agencies (NGOs), galleries and artists enhanced the benefits of arts education. They commented partner agencies "generally agree that the results [of the arts programmes] are positive back in the school and in the community. Arts programming is educational but is not always only located in a school. The educator is often an artist aided by one of the partners."

The involvement of partnerships artist/education as a valuable way to enhance student attitude was also evident in data from Australia, Colombia, New Zealand, UK, USA, and Finland. In the latter country the project *Girls, boys and 'gender play'*, reportedly provides an example of how partnerships between schools, museums and local authorities can be fostered through the Internet. Schools and museums were asked to join the project via Internet. It was required that in every local project there were two partners, school and museum – or regional environmental centre. There were 216 local projects and over a hundred Unesco Associated schools. Altogether 400 schools, 500 teachers, 65 museums and 15 organisations in 70 municipalities participated in the project. *The Association of Finish Local and Regional Authorities* indicated that in 87% of municipalities, the cultural sector was working with schools. The project involved both the development of instructional material and inservice teacher education.

Badu Island Primary School – participating in the 100% in Control Croc Festival in Thursday Island (Australia) – July 2005. Photo courtesy of Peter Sjoquist.

The reported results were:

> Teachers learned to work with experts out of school and experts learned to work with school teachers and pupils ... Pupils were active in the local projects and in their opinion workshops, exhibitions, study trips and visitors in school were good ways to learn. Especially they liked idea of learning by doing (work of arts, making their own learning material). Also children's and young people's skills to work co-operatively increased.

In Singapore, the observation was made that public experiences outside the school context (such as visits to galleries, public exhibitions, performance and events) were an important part of the process of building positive attitudes and confidence in the children. These additional 'extension' arts activities were popular and added to the overall success of arts education. For example:

> The Paris trip in 2003 had a positive influence over the students which saw a vast improvement in their attitude towards art. This change in attitude was evident in their enthusiasm during the participation in other school projects (*Craft & Food Fair*). The quality of post-trip art works

was of higher standards and more experimental as the students were more receptive towards the use of various mediums and presentation styles. The annual Craft and Food Fair was an event which demonstrated a whole-school approach in its contribution to the arts. Every student (from every level and stream) demonstrated optimistic attitude whilst making craft works for sale during the fair. Also the students' attendance for the arts enrichment programme had been good, especially for the *Normal Technical* (NT) stream. Sec 1-3 (NT) students showed high level of enthusiasm and participation in the *Percussion Workshop*.

A significant number of the qualitative responses described the positive impact of the arts on building a sense of democratic and social 'selves' within the children. In several examples given, the arts were closely linked to values education and the development of positive social behaviours. For instance, in Barbados it was observed that "values education is intrinsic to arts education." and that participation in the arts nurtured "co-operation, respect, responsibility, tolerance, and appreciation" within the learning process. This aspect of arts education has been formalised within the design of the general school curriculum in Colombia. For example:

> The Ministry of Education began in recent years the process of constructing a series of basic standards for teaching *Democratic Competences* in primary and secondary schools. Democratic competences are conceived as a set of necessary cognitive, emotional and communicational abilities and related knowledge for peaceful coexistence. Children and young people are provided with tools that help them to relate harmoniously to each other within respect of differences implied in a plural society like ours. Art is often used as a vehicle for teaching Democratic Competences. Examples of projects with this approach are: *Plan Nacional de la Música para la Convivencia, Incolballet, Colegio del Cuerpo, Teatro Itinerante del Sol,* and other experiences. These projects belong to the sphere of non-formal education.

It was acknowledged that the chance for students to present and explain their artistic projects and the participation in reflective thinking associated with the presentation of artistic projects greatly enhanced students' confidence. This process of feedback and reflection was seen to be a major contributing factor in improving student learning and confidence. The following example comes from Singapore:

> After returning from the 2004 Paris trip, which was a morale and confidence booster for the art students, the students embarked on yet another project, a full-scale art exhibition involving 4 other schools at the *Singapore Asian Civilisation Museum*. [In another example] Teachers gave feedback that the Speech & Drama training programmes helped students

to build up their confidence in public speaking, both in class and on stage. [In another example] Secondary students were deployed as event MCs for school functions.

These findings were also observed in Barbados where it was noted that there was a great enthusiasm for drama and performance and that the students are "eager to participate. Shy students gradually become less introverted. Expression is allowed and encouraged based on students' interests and aptitude of the various art-forms." Drama was seen to be a particularly important aspect of arts education in terms of building students' confidence.

In Senegal it was noted that students involved in arts classes were more initiative, overcame timidity and were more willing to effectively express themselves in public. Similarly, substantial studies in Finland suggest that drama gives young people "different ways to express" themselves. Research from Canada affirms that arts education increased self confidence. These findings were also evident in studies conducted in the Netherlands and Austria, while in China it was noted that arts projects gave young people the opportunity to perform in front of an audience had a positive impact on children's confidence levels. A number of respondents also commented that the process of presentation encouraged greater pupil reflection. For example, Austrian and Australian research both indicate that the development of presentational skills instigated greater personal reflection and an increase in the critical stance adopted by students towards their artistic work.

In other national systems, such as Spain, the attitudes have been maintained almost in spite of the lack of arts education provisions. It was described that in Spain it was almost impossible to continue to maintain the development of artistic attitudes and social experiences because of the lack of support given to the arts in schools. Despite this, it was noted that artistic attitudes still survive through, "small associations that intend in a great effort, to maintain [an artistic attitude] and to live the [artistic] spirit and the capacity to think".

While the majority of responding countries noted enhanced individual attitude and confidence, a similar percent (80%) of countries commented that arts education directly enhanced social and cultural understanding within the school and broader community. In Nigeria it was noted that arts education provided an opportunity for young people to mix freely with "others regardless of age, colour and status" and that it developed the students culturally as "they are able to appreciate the value of other people's culture." It was considered in Nigeria that this cultural diffusion was made possible through the exhibition of the students' artworks. In Singapore, the arts were used directly as a way to raise funds that were distributed to poor groups within the community. This country also indicated that the exposure to diverse art forms led to greater cultural understanding, as evident in the following example:

The broad range of Arts Exposure (performances for large audiences during assembly) and Art experiences (eg. *Kolam* making workshop) exposed students from various ethnic groups to each others' cultural heritage, which contributed to the student's cultural development in school. The school has 3 ethnic dance groups, namely the Malay, Chinese and Indian Dance Club. During *National Day Celebration*, dancers from the 3 dance clubs would take the initiative to choreograph together an ethnic fusion dance item. During the process of choreographing and practising, students from various ethnic groups would have the opportunity to learn and to appreciate each others' dance forms.

In Barbados, there is a strong link between the arts programmes in school and local and national cultural and religious festivals and events. For example, schools are "involved in national cultural events: [such as] *Crop Over, Pan Yard Lines, Jazz Festival, Holders Hill Theatre Festival*, both as performers and audience."

Young performers from the state of Niedersachsen, Germany, on stage at the 20th Schools' Theatre Festival in Stuttgart, 2004, organized by the German National Drama and Theatre Education Association, Bundesverband Darstellendes Spiel. Photo courtesy of Dan Baron Cohen.

In the USA, a number of substantial studies have been conducted into the impact of the arts on social development. These studies indicate a strong correlation between positive social and cultural awareness and participation in the arts. Within the USA, arts education researchers have studied social development through the arts:

> Studies conducted by Steve Seidel at *Harvard*, Shirley Brice Heath at *Stanford*, and Rob Horowitz at *Colombia* universities appear in the document *Champions of Change* and the *Coming Up Taller Awards* (see www.cominguptaller.org/new.html) acknowledge the role of the arts in building social responsibility.

Other countries made reference to generic social skills fostered through arts education. For example, in the Netherlands it was noted that involvement in quality arts education developed within students the skills to "learn to work together, to deal with others and to communicate in order to produce a result." Results similar to these were also apparent in the UK, Canadian and Australian research where it was noted that arts education had contributed to well-being in Aboriginal and culturally diverse communities. In these situations arts education had engendered "healing effects, increasing awareness, understanding, pride and celebration". Within these communities art education extended beyond the classroom to generally infuse community life with the arts. In this way, it was not strictly about the contribution of school-based art education, but rather the more holistic inclusion of arts into daily life.

Within Canada, there were also a number of arts companies specifically designed to address issues of culture and social diversity and these groups were largely community based and worked very closely with schools. In Spain, there were some travelling performance groups that specifically addressed issues of cultural diversity and they presented performances at "*days multitematicas*". This was also the case in Denmark where arts and cultural funding had been used to make performance and exhibitions accessible to all children and their communities.

In Germany, the process of social and cultural development was formally documented through the *'Kompetenznachweis Kultur'* (Cultural Competency Record) and the implementation of after-school culture and arts education projects "showed clearly the effects on students' social and cultural development".

Similarly, studies from Colombia indicate that "cultural heritage is most effectively generated throughs artistic (re) production." The best example of this is from Gobernación Norte de Santander in Colombia. This territory in the north-east frontier of Colombia and Venezuela based has a population of 1,435,237 with 26% of the population in rural settings and 74% set in the cities with a 45% of basic needs unfulfilled through the predominantly mining and agricultural economy. For more than 50 years this region rich in natural resources has been "humbled by armed conflict, creating high levels of violence and forced displacements." There are indications that these problems can – at least partially – be addressed through arts education. The project in Norte de Santander allows "junction spaces for local inter-institutional meeting". The regions develop plans for artistic and cultural activities and, at the national level, develop actions that enable the citizens to "articulate, make stronger and consolidate" the formation processes generated at the local level. The schools become an "alternate space" within the regions that encourage "the young population – children and teenagers – to creatively and constructively use free time as an alternate expression of their social reality. Sometimes all good things go together."

Qualitative comments from Senegal also highlight the important social and cultural impact that can result from achieving recognition for artistic endeavours. In the Senegalese example it is suggested that:

> The expression of artistic talent often contributes to social recognition and inspires admiration. Obtaining a distinction, be it within the class or at national or international level, always has a cultural and social impact on the winner's environment. The media also make this impact greater.

Arts education and the community

- Arts education plays a major role in community and cultural development and as such should hold a major role within formal education curricula
- Quality arts education within schools can lead to social, economic and educational improvements within communities
- Community links add to the success of art programmes
- Performances and public presentation of arts-rich curricula help build positive perceptions of the individual, the school and the community

The research across a number of countries indicated that partnerships and closer links between arts education and the arts and cultural community enhanced the value for arts-rich education and had also directly and indirectly led to the establishment of a number of professional performance and artist groups working primarily in education and community contexts.

The data clearly indicates that the fostering of a sense of community and cultural citizenship is a key role played by art education. Of all the different types of benefits attributed to quality arts education, of most significance is the area of community and cultural development. A total of 87% of countries said that arts education had improved community bonds and 88% of respondents stated that arts education had improved cultural dialogue and the understanding of different cultures. More specifically, 80% said that art education had led to more community and family involvement in education. The magnitude of these figures, suggest that arts education plays a major role in community and cultural development and as such should hold a major role within formal education curricula. The qualitative data points to extensive and varied models of community building and engagement generated by arts education. The qualitative comments also suggest that strong cultural communities can both enrich – and be enriched by – arts education programmes.

In the USA issues of community development have been reported on at a national level. These studies reaffirm the role of arts education in promoting sustainable communities.

> These issues [issues of arts education and community development] are addressed in two publications: *The Community, Culture and Globalization* commissioned by *The Rockefeller Foundation* and edited by Don Adams and Arlene Goldbard and Creative Community: *The Art of Cultural Development* by Adams and Goldbard. There is also a new report on community arts: *The State of the Field of Community Cultural Development: Something New Emerges* http://www.communityarts.net/ readingroom/archive/canreport/

The three studies referred to above take a broad view of the role of arts education in building communities within the USA context. These results were also apparent in the national forum on *Promoting the Value of the Arts* in Australia and other fora held in New Zealand, England and Scotland. In Glasgow, for example, a focus on art education (particularly in the area of design) was attributed in transforming the city into a more creative and progressive community. A number of case studies from the English, *Creative Partnerships* projects strongly indicate the role of quality arts education in regenerating communities and building effective education and community partnerships that have clear mutual benefits for both the schools and the community.

In the qualitative data there were many examples of more small scale – but equally significant – ways arts education projects had encouraged closer links between the school, community and family. For example, in Singapore the *Annual Craft & Food Fair* saw an increase in parents' involvement (helping students in the making of craft works for fund raising and even setting up of their own *Parents' Support* food & craft stalls) and public attendance. Similarly, in Hong Kong schools usually invite parents or neighbouring schools to their performances, hence involving parents and the community as well.

In Australia, there was substantial qualitative evidence of family and community involvement in arts and education through the *Remote Music Delivery* programme, from *Charles Darwin University* that provided remote indigenous communities with music education. This programme was based on substantial involvement of indigenous community musicians in the design and implementation of a music programme within schools and found that the partnership between the arts and education led directly to increased family and parental involvement in their children's school community and daily education processes.

Likewise, in Germany, cultural and arts education projects inside and outside "schools for young people in deprived city areas very often bring the families of the youngsters in contact with the arts for the first time."

Many of the countries saw community links as being a vital part of successful arts education programmes. In Austria, quality arts programmes involve schools working with artists and the presentation of the work within a community context. Similarly, in the Netherlands, art is to be seen and shared and so it stimulates family and community to get involved in education. In Colombia most of the art projects developed stress pedagogic or educative processes that involve the participation of family and community. The Colombian experience suggests that:

> These processes [involving community] have become themselves part of the creative activity and its relation with the public gains everyday more and more relevance. It is important to emphasize that the complex dynamics of our country makes family and community the main vehicles of transmission of traditional expressions of the arts and culture, through informal circuits. In these complex circumstances informal cultural education intertwines with formal education.

This situation is similar in Senegal where arts education allows "families and communities to see the status of various aspects of their local culture improved (songs, dances, costumes, housing). This contributes to the building and strengthening of the pupil's identity as well as of the cultural identity of the community." This was mainly achieved through an arts and culture programme in Senegal:

> Initiated within the frame of the Arts Education programme for the promotion of arts and the culture of citizenship at school, the '*Educ'Art*' Carnival is a 'fashion show' taking place in the streets of Dakar. Boys and girls are invited to dress up with fantastic costumes, make-up, hairdo and accessories made by themselves during the Arts Education classes. They are then invited to parade in the streets, accompanied by songs, dances and instrumental music. Artists take part to the project as well.

The purpose is to promote the playful, aesthetic, cultural and social dimensions of Arts Education. The 'Educ'Art' Carnival appears as a very effective way to promote the social function of school. That's why social themes have been chosen for the first two editions: the promotion of teenagers' rights in 2003, and now *"Tlibé"'*, a plea for difficult childhood.

In Nigeria, it was noted that increased art education in the schools had led renewed interest in traditional crafts within the communities and that this was beginning to have a positive effect on the economies of a number of local communities.

Arts education appears to operate very effectively to bring parents and the community into the educational school settings, but it is also clear that arts education projects serve as an effective way to extend the reach of educational programmes into the community. For example, in Singapore, school-based performing arts groups were actively involved in community events. They contributed to "band performances for *Yio Chu Kang Community Centre's Opening Ceremony* and *Christmas Bash, Fringe Performances at Sentosa* and the *National Day Parade*. These events resulted in the schools being identified as schools of excellence and generally built the prestige and desirability of the schools. This in turn enhanced the allure of the community as being a 'good place to live'.

In Barbados, arts education was seen to foster lifelong learning and community links. For example, "students graduate from dancing in schools and continue to dance with the community dance schools." It was stated that, "Families [in Barbados] are committed to assist with costuming, make-up, box office, transportation." In Colombia, community involvement has been embedded as a core requirement of curriculum reform in music education. As one of its lines of action, the *Plan Nacional de Música para la Convivencia* promotes the participation of the community in the processes of creation and sustainability of music schools in different practices. The programme encourages the organization of the community around their music schools hence creating community bonds which strongly support artistic development of children and young people.

The chance to present artistic achievement in a community context was also seen to be a way of building students' identity and confidence. In for example:

> The product generated by ways of the teaching of the arts and the development of the cultural activities have permitted students to approach the community with greater confidence in their artistic expressions. [Community performances] are demanded by the children and the community and enjoyment is gained from participating actively in the monthly or annual samples [that are presented]. These artistic schools are used to being open to the community to share with them their achievements.

Community involvement was also seen as a way of building racial harmony within the school and the community and acknowledging identity and cultural difference. This aspect was identifies through substantial studies conducted in the UK.

> The *Ofsted* report *Improving City Schools* (HMI, 2003) reported that the arts curriculum in many of the primary and secondary schools visited was designed to take full advantage of the richness provided by cultural diversity. Strong links with parents and local culturally diverse arts organisations was noted. Supporting, developing and extending local cultures were noted by one teacher to be a feature of their success.

> Downing et al (2003) asked teachers and head teachers to rank the five most important purposes for teaching the arts in their school. One of the options was 'understanding and respecting other cultures'. 23% of head teachers and 20% of teachers ranked this in their five most important purposes for arts education. This was a moderate result when compared to the other 17 choices.

> Harland et al (2000) investigated developments in awareness and understanding of the cultural domain, including greater awareness of different cultural traditions. Teachers responded that all art-forms impacted positively on cultural awareness. Both in schools with high proportions of children from ethnic minorities and those with low proportions, the arts were considered important in developing young people's attitudes towards a multiethnic and multicultural society. Teachers felt it was important to learn about one's own culture, as well as those of other people. Like teachers, students felt that all art-forms contributed to an awareness of other cultures.

In Germany and Finland, specific programmes link arts education with cultural understanding.

> [In Finland] *The University of Art and Design* and the *University of Music* collaborated with the *City of Helsinki* to create a wonderful project in a school, where there are many refugees and immigrants. The results of this project were very positive. The whole atmosphere in the school changed and the schoolwork was far more interesting for the foreigners. The multicultural aspect is written very strongly into the national core curriculum. Senior advisors are taking care of UNESCO associated schools. The schools are working on these topics, too.

In Germany it was noted that in schools and out of schools cultural and arts educa-tion projects frequently choose an 'intercultural' theme or subject because of the different ethnic backgrounds of pupils and youngsters in their class or group.

Arts education projects had also provided an avenue for cultural exchanges between teachers and children. In Barbados, the project method adopted to teach arts education gives students the opportunity to explore other people's and cultures. Barbados recently hosted 2 groups of teachers from U.K. on cultural visits to explore arts education in Barbadian schools. Additionally, the *African Caribbean Film Festival* promotes the exchange of dialogue between film makers and Barbadian students.

The Ministry of Education in Colombia is developing a project in *Ethnoeducación* in which students of different ethnic origins learn in their own language or dialect. "The programmes that use arts education as a vehicle for teaching *Democratic Competences* and promote in the students the idea of intercultural dialogue." This is significant within education in Colombia in terms of the plurality of this particular society.

In other examples, community involvement is more spasmodic. For example, within Finland, community involvement in arts education is very good in some communities but poor in others. In situations where there are strong relationships between schools and the community there are "cultural centres, special cultural programmes, school cinemas and out-of-school arts schools, passport system to attend cultural evens, museums and so on". In building these strong relationships, it is acknowledged that family background and parents' own lack of exposure to arts education negatively impacts on community and family involvement in arts educa-tion.

In Spain, for example, there is generally only family and community involvement when there is a special event, for religious or national celebrations, but these do not translate into increased parental or community support for arts education. In Spain there are "very few cultural centres that exchange information with children and youths of other countries, with other mentalities and cultures." The Spanish data suggests that this is a concerning omission in their education, given the increasingly global nature of the world.

Key to enhanced community and arts education partnerships appears to be the building of sustained relationships with artists, galleries and other arts and cultural groups and organisations. In Nigeria, they are designing programmes which take arts education into the community. Through interacting with artists, visiting exhibitions, participating in workshops and attending fieldtrips, strong community links have been forged with school-based arts education programmes. Similarly,

Singaporean schools pro-actively source arts partners to collaborate in school projects. These partnerships strengthened community bonds. For example, "the school managed to close a deal to have the school's art exhibition hosted at the *Singapore Asian Civilisation Museum* over the next three years" and "the school's growing strength in the performing arts led to many invitations to support local community events." In a very different community context, Indigenous elders are harnessed in the delivery of art education programmes in remote areas of Australia.

Closer links between arts education and the arts and cultural community has also directly led to the establishment of a number of professional performance and artist groups who work primarily in education and community contexts. In Australia there are many performance groups whose entire programme is aimed at developing the arts in schools and the community. In Barbados, there has been a "surge of community performance groups, supported by the business community within respective districts" and "the churches have embraced the Performing Arts as a Ministry primarily comprising the youth."

In conclusion, linking education and the community seems to be a major effect of arts education. Research studies in England indicate that this is a substantial benefit of the full inclusion of arts education in the compulsory education curriculum:

> Head teachers were asked by Downing et al (2003) what were the benefits of arts to the school and to pupils. A common response to this question was that the arts can help schools to reach out to their local communities. One school is quoted mentioning that they had a low profile in their community but by using the arts these are helping to raise that school profile. The "Space for Sport and Arts" scheme and "Specialist Arts Colleges" contribute to building ties between schools and their local communities.

The benefits of the arts as building the profile of a school was also apparent in data from Canada, where it was suggested that, the arts are always featured in the marketing of schools to parents and communities. They are also integral to the "community life of a school."

Arts education, imagination and creativity

- Creativity and imagination can be nurtured through arts-based processes
- Poor quality arts education or no arts education may inhibit the development of creativity and imagination
- Arts education can instigate more creative and interesting approaches to teaching

In quality arts-rich education the relationship between teachers and students is collaborative and trusting. Within this context it is possible to provide a climate that may engender more creative and imaginative learning outcomes. However, the extensive research which underpins this global research analysis cautions that there is little evidence to support the idea that the arts alone – or even predominantly – can be considered to directly impact in the areas of creativity and imagination. While it has been a long held belief that the arts build creativity and imagination with children, there was limited empirical evidence to support this as a conclusive finding of this report. It could be said that there is a lack of understanding of the terms *creativity* and *imagination* and comparative and empirical data is difficult to obtain.

The issue of creativity and imagination resulted in the most diverse responses of any area of the research. While the general consensus identified research that supported the view that arts education engendered creativity and imagination, there was also the widely held view that these attributes can be nurtured through the arts, but not directly taught. This is underlined by a comment from a Canadian respondent, "personally, I don't think you teach imagination as much as you create a free, open, non-judgemental environment with many opportunities to explore imagination."

This view was also mirrored from results of research conducted in England where students were interviewed about imagination and the arts:

> Harland et al (2000) sought pupils' views on the development of imagination in arts education. Many pupils referred to imagination as an effect of arts education. Imagination was considered in terms of coming up with own ideas, as well as interpreting other artists' work and mixing this with own ideas. Pupils' talked about developing imagination through a sense of freedom and spontaneity. The emphasis in the pupils' comments was on imaginative and creative processes, not on the product of arts education.

There was also a view that an overemphasis on creativity and imagination may have been detrimental to sustained art education, where these aims had been used to justify approaches that lack rigor and fail to provide students with the cognitive and discipline-based skills needed to participate fully in the arts.

The quantitative data indicates that while 75% of countries acknowledged that creativity was enhanced through quality arts education, a relatively high 25% of responding countries felt there were little or no connection between arts education and the development of creativity and imagination.

Vogler Quartet in Sligo Pilot Project 1999-2004. Music education from classroom work-shops with the Vogler. Image courtesy of Mary McAuliffe, County Sligo Arts Officer, Ireland.

These figures are interesting, as creativity and imagination are traditionally seen to be the main reason for the inclusion of arts within the school curriculum. Given the data from this research, it seems far more significant that the arts contribute to cultural and community development and that the development of imagination and creativity – while still significant – is of less overall importance.

Significantly, creativity and imagination were perceived as teaching and learning methods, rather than content. So, for instance, an arts-based approach to learning is likely to be more original, engaging, open-ended and pupil-centred. Conversely, in school systems such as Republic of Seychelles, more creative approaches to teaching and learning methods were considered to be dangerous and anti-social. In this system, "creativity is more or less considered, in practice, as a deviant, anti-social behaviour whether displayed by a pupil or a teacher. Natural curiosity may be considered as mischief-making."

In Barbados and England, specific programmes have been developed to build creativity and imagination within overall approaches to learning. The PEACE programme in Barbados trained teachers to use drama strategies to enhance the teaching/learning process in all subject areas. In England there are many examples of attempts to use more creative based methods of learning:

130

The Arts Council's Creative Partnerships programme provides school children across England with the opportunity to develop creativity in learning and to take part in cultural activities of the highest quality. Some of this work is through arts education. The research programme associated with Creative Partnerships will be investigating this; however no report is available at this time.

Arts Education in Secondary Schools: Effects and Effectiveness (Harland et al, 2000) investigated the development of creativity and thinking skills. Numerous responses were given by both teachers and pupils in relation to the outcome of creativity from arts education lessons. For pupils, creativity, imagination and experimentation was about using their own ideas. Creativity was frequently recognised as an effect of arts education; however pupils had a very wide definition of creativity. There was no progressive or sequential thought to how pupils recognised the development of creativity.

Projects and institutions like *Colegio del Cuerpo, Taller del Parque, Imaginando Nuestra Imagen, Mafalda and Academia de Arte Guerrero* in Colombia focus on the development of students' imagination. Generally speaking, the academic world suggests a strong connection between arts education and the development of imagination and creativity but there were limited statistics or case studies that give a precise answer to the question.

In Germany, Finland and Austria, respondents reported anecdotally how arts education had given rise to more creative and interesting approaches to teaching. For example, the projects in Finland have shown "that creativity has increased by Generalist Teachers and among other teachers as well (especially in the project The Oak of Finland)". Similarly, in Austria it was noted that there are "quite fascinating results but we do not have a comprehensive concept of creativity in schools by which to compare these results". In Germany they also noticed that the teachers' approaches to the pupils altered to become more facilitation oriented. The Finish examples pointed to the way enhanced art education experiences built the creative capabilities of generalist teachers. It should also be noted, that while many countries experienced these sorts of changes, there was consensus that there was a lack of understanding of the terms creativity and imagination and this meant that comparative and empirical data was difficult to obtain.

In several countries, creativity and imagination were actually perceived to be adversely effected by poor quality arts eduction programmes. In Australia the comment was made that:

Many arts education programmes actually hinder creativity; by not providing a developmentally appropriate toolkit of skills with which to explore creative expression, and by not providing opportunities, time, or frameworks which scaffold creative expression. I am concerned that many arts education programmes discourage the active and creative use of imagination, in the demands to conform to a standard form of artistic expression.

Similarly, it was noted in Austria and the Netherlands, that while creativity and imagination could be engendered through the arts, this was generally not the case, and even where it was apparent in some instances, these were poorly researched and evaluated to determine the real nature of the learning that was occurring

Despite these reservations, in countries such as Canada, where substantial studies in this field have been conducted, the relationship between arts education and creativity and imagination appears to be direct and causal. The Canadian response, built on the findings of a number of research studies, suggests "almost all studies report such findings". Education in creative and imaginative approaches was also a feature of the Canadian system. For example, "most teacher education extra-curricular programmes [in Canada] rely on the arts. Student services at my institution run such art-focussed groups for teacher education candidates."

In Colombia, the difficulties experienced in the country seem to have ironically led to higher levels of creativity but this 'natural creativity' is not effectively engaged within the formal school context:

Creativity flourishes in most of the Colombian territory, giving live to the cultural diversity of music, visual arts, dance, literature, and other art practices, and it is generated from a strong multicultural heritage. The natural flow of creativity in Colombia is strongly related to the difficulties that Colombians have to face in periods of crisis, and is promoted specially in an informal circuit. This creativity potential is rarely developed and the talent of children and young people reaches its maturity only in exceptional cases. This has also the effect of rendering the activity of art unsustainable. Few examples of particular projects can be given, such as the programmes developed by the *Universidad de Antioquia* jointly with the *Cultural Office of Norte de Santander* in which teachers are being trained to teach creativity at school.

While the results on the impact of the arts on imagination and creativity are largely anecdotal and could not be considered causal, empirical evidence suggests that the expansion of arts-rich education within general education, or as an adjunct to education within the informal education sector had a marked impact on children's general health, well-being and positive social engagement.

Arts education, health and well-being

- There was a positive benefit to health and well-being by young people engaging in quality arts education
- Arts education involves learning processes that are structurally different from other disciplines within the curriculum

There was strong evidence within a wide variety of educational contexts that quality arts-rich education served to counteract student alienation and reinvigorate teachers' enthusiasm. It was generally the case that arts teachers, artists and those teachers who employ arts-based teaching methodologies are perceived to be more approachable, supportive and encouraging than general teachers. It was also evidenced that arts-rich programmes may have therapeutic impacts on alienated students and those with special physical, mental, behavioural and/or learning needs. While these results are noted very consistently across and number of international case studies, it is more difficult to make causal assumptions for these observations.

It appears that arts-rich programmes encourage more focused classroom interactions, greater concentration during school and more consistent school attendance – especially in boys and marginalised students. To be able to make this a definitive finding, more research would needed into the possible connections between arts education, cognitive development and health and well-being impacts for young people.

A number of innovative projects exist around the world for using the arts to enhance the education received by students with special needs and/or with disabilities. For example, the *"I can do it"* project in Mongolia has developed arts curriculum with a special focus on children with disabilities and their families.

In recent years, art educators have been looking to the positive benefits of arts education on the health and well-being of young people. The focus has been on the way projects such as CAPE in the USA, and EAPI in Australia might help to address issues of alienation, identity and health in 'at risk' young people. The results of the quantitative data suggest that 65% of countries noted a positive benefit to health and well-being by young people engaging in quality arts education.

There was also though a relatively high level (31%) of respondents who disagreed that arts contributed to well-being or who had inadequate research findings to give an informed opinion. This deviation suggests that more research is needed into the possible connections between arts education and health and well-being impacts for young people.

Given this caveat, many countries reported both anecdotally and in terms of re-search conducted of a positive correlation between arts education programmes in schools and the positive well-being of the pupils. This connection tended to be made in three main ways.

Firstly that the nature of artistic processes were more creative and led to greater mental acuity and confidence; the second that arts education involved building strong positive relationships that assisted pupil well-being; and, thirdly, that there were therapeutic benefits of art education, especially on the more disadvantaged groups within the school environment.

A pertinent example of this type was a project in Finland. A case study from Finland was reported as follows:

> In Helsinki Polytechnic the special aim was to use drama and digital art in the group of school drop-outs, and to develop a network of NGO's and educational institutions to allow mobility of students and for volunteers to develop expertise of working with excluded groups. The [drama] ses-sions were integrated into the curriculum. For the pupils the drama was a tool to express their future hopes and to look at themselves as individuals and to support identity-building and self-esteem. The project also aimed to promote and support the group behaviour… All the participants in the projects learned to work together – social workers, social and healthcare students, theatre students and teachers.

This finding is not culture specific or necessarily dependent upon a high level of socioeconomic development. Indeed similar findings have been reported from Africa. A wonderful example of this is *The Empire* in Senegal. Based in a former open-air cinema in Dakar, the project was set up to "improve the level and quality of life of the children by favouring their social integration through the arts." After a complete renovation of the cinema, the project was inaugurated on May 17th 2002, within the framework of the *Arts Biennial*. Children from the streets, mostly socially excluded boys aged 5 to 16, with "a history of violence, precariousness and loneliness", were the target-group for the Empire. By attracting these youths, the Empire offers:

- Accommodation (someone to talk to, a roof, health, social and educational sup-port, visits, apprenticeship);
- Training (computer science, Internet, painting, batik, music, drama, dance, cinema, radio and TV, sports);
- Exchanges with foreign structures following the same goals.

The results were impressive, showing that "conformity with the arts education policy promoted solidarity and children's rights. The Empire provided a socio-cultural centre for children, and increased possibilities for educational experimentation, social integration, protection against violence and the risks of marginalization."

The qualitative data suggests that through arts education, students are being creative and this contributes to making pupils more mentally alert. It was also suggested that arts education builds reflectivity and allows young people to get "in contact with their personality". This has a favourable impact on the way pupils treat themselves and form self-identities.

In many countries, arts education was seen to involve learning processes that were structurally different from other parts of the curriculum. Arts education is often perceived as being "an escape from continual rigours of rote" (Republic of Seychelles). There are some positive examples of improvement in the mental health of young people brought about by participating in arts projects which break the routines of the school curriculum (Austria). In Hong Kong it was noted that effective arts education projects required critical and creative thinking and physical coordination. It was particularly mentioned that "even children in special education schools benefit from the projects". It was also revealed that most art teachers tended to be well-regarded by pupils in that they are of lower esteem – "not proper teachers – than, say, a Maths or French teacher, and younger, but are more accessible on a human level (like an elder brother/sister)". It could be inferred from this data that art teachers are generally perceived to be more approachable, supportive and encouraging.

The well-being benefits of arts education seem to be particularly felt by those pupils traditionally alienated from the school system. In Singapore, it was noted that creating an aesthetically enhanced environment and incorporating extensive arts programmes into the curriculum produced particular benefit to students from the lower group of SES (social economic status). These students no longer had the mental perception that art was only accessible and appreciated by the privileged students. Similarly, Australian art programmes implemented within 'special schools', youth detention centres and refugee settings have all noted benefits in this area.

In England, "Harland et al (2000) concluded that one effect of arts education involvement was as therapy. Both teachers and pupils testified to this effect and in particular the calming effect on a pupil's temperament or a means of stress relief". From the pupils' perspective, involvement in the arts provided a release from the stresses of everyday life and from the stress of other lessons. Correspondingly, in Senegal it was noted that:

> Genuine arts education improves sensitivity as well as the mental and physical health of individuals. It is even more obvious when it comes to the education of mentally or physically handicapped children. The *Sene-*

galese Psychiatric Hospital, the *National Verbotonal Centre* and the *National Centre for the Education and Rehabilitation of the Physically Handicapped* often call on arts education teachers." A Senegalese visual arts teacher is going to specialise in Art-Therapy. The events organized in these institutions are very moving and perfectly illustrate the 'miracle' at work in such an educational approach. Let's not forget either the existence of traditional therapeutic approaches using costumes, music, dances, trances, etc.

These therapeutic and rehabilitation approaches to art education have been used extensively in Canada as part of that country's anti-bullying and anti-racism strategies. In Finland, arts education is widely used in hospitals. A number of countries also mentioned that arts therapy courses have become popular post-graduate options for teachers and that several doctoral dissertations are being completed looking at the therapeutic impact of the arts. The results of this work should provide substantial documentation to inform policy makers in the future.

Allied to the issue of pupil well-being and health was the way in which art education might build greater concentration and focus in schools. The response to this question in the quantitative section of the survey suggests that this is the least well understood aspect of arts education. There was very limited research on the way arts education might promote cognitive skills and improved concentration and intellectual acuity. Only 43% of countries saw this as something that was developed through arts education. A large (48%) percent of respondents could not find any research to either support or refute this within their country, while 9% of respondents did not think that art education enhanced student focus or concentration. Given these figures, it suggests that further research is warranted in this aspect of arts education.

In Australia, there are some studies that indicate arts education programmes have assisted in developing greater concentration and more focus in pupils. The EAPI projects indicated that participation in the arts – despite the teachers' preconceived idea that it would make pupils less settled and more disruptive – actually led to more focused classroom interactions, greater concentration during school and greater attendance to intellectual development. This evidence was obtained through five substantial studies conducted in Australia over an 18-month period and used both qualitative information obtained from teachers and children and quantitative measures from attendance records and the like.

Also in Australia, the *Boys Business* arts project for male students showed that involvement in arts education resulted in less disruptive behaviour and greater focus. The comment was made that "arts education teaches students 'How to think' rather than 'what to think' and so we see ample evidence of better concentration."

The extensive Australian studies suggest that arts education leads to increased attention or concentration span and the ability to complete a learning task, as observable outcomes of students' participation. Research conducted in CAPE (USA) and the widespread research by Shirley Brice-Heath indicates similar findings.

Other countries reported anecdotal evidence that the arts led to greater concentration and intellectual capabilities. For example in Spain it was noted that literature and painting were particularly able to promote higher order intellectual and thinking skills. In China, it was seen that the rigour of developing and performing drama, musical and other arts presentations required significant levels of focus and concentration and the transfer of these skills led to greater overall school achievement. While this evidence is encouraging, more substantial studies are needed in the area of cognitive development and arts.

Arts education and technology

- Arts education develops ICT literacies and technical skills
- Arts-based programmes should use industry standard software and hardware
- Teachers need more training in ICT literacies and skills relevant to the arts
- Arts education needs to be given greater access to technology, especially in the economic developing countries

The area of ICT literacy and technology rates highly in the agendas of most education systems around the world. It is therefore of interest to ascertain the extent to which arts education might develop these skills within young people. The quantitative and qualitative data suggests that – where computers are readily available to arts educators and pupils – arts education has contributed significantly to teaching information and communications technologies (ICT), computer skills and technology skills. In 63% of countries arts education had actively developed ICT literacies and technical competencies in their pupils.

In countries such as Australia, New Zealand, Canada, Spain, Germany, USA, China and England where there is high computer usage in schools, arts education was seen as being a key part of ICT literacy programmes. In Australia, for example, computer applications are a core part of arts education. Arts education programmes in Australia and New Zealand routinely use industry standard hardware and software, as well as presentation and communications software. Similarly, in Canada, visual arts and music have led the ICT revolution and technology is now being expanded into the dance and drama areas. In Finland, the visual arts and music make extensive and creative use of ICT within their design and implementation. IT literacy is an important subject in the core arts curriculum.

A substantial evidence base is being gathered in England to provide case studies of the impact of ICT in arts education. Studies conducted in 2003 indicate a strong connection between arts-rich education and the extensive and imaginative use of ICT, as the following analysis suggests:

> *Keys to Imagination: ICT in Art Education* (Davies et al, 2003) involved a series of case study school visits made in February and March 2003, along with a review of current and recent literature and survey data. The study found that while there are undoubtedly areas of practice which are effective and occasionally inspirational, the research points to a disappointing picture with little consolidated progress in effective integration of ICT into art and design education in schools. In some schools ICT is still seen as developing office-based skills, and thus many art and design teachers do not see the use of ICT as relevant to their subject area. Where used, the technology generally facilitates the use of ideas and not the focus of work.

> During an investigation into arts-rich schools (QCA, 2002) in England, the most sited area for development by Head Teachers was ICT and the arts. There was general dissatisfaction with software and advice, but they had a good understanding of the opportunities for teaching and learning ICT could offer.

The issue of teacher education in IT and ICT literacies is an important issue for art education. As was indicated in the results from England, teachers in arts education may lack personal skills in these areas. This was noted in the qualitative data from Germany and Austria, where it was felt that the broader adoption of IT into the arts curricula was limited by the need to develop technology skills among arts education teachers.

In countries such as Nigeria, it was considered that arts education programmes had increased ICT literacy but the full impact of this had been constrained by a lack of computers, especially in government funded schools and even greater lack of computers made available to arts education. This was a similar issue in the Republic of the Seychelles, where only a handful of students get access to computers.

The art are not just about aesthetics, they also provide an effective means of enhancing the innovative use of ICT. Though, this only happens if the arts teachers are given access to computers and gain competence in their use. However, these benefits – and the other benefits highlighted in this chapter – are not the reason for teaching art education. The arts have an intrinsic value and a higher purpose, namely to ensure that children flourish and that we live our lives to the full.

Chapter 8:
Conclusions and future directions

Introduction

This global research indicated that while advocacy to include arts as part of education policy has largely been successful, this has not led to wide scale implementation of quality arts programmes at the school level. The current situation sees global monitoring and reporting on educational standards within literacy, mathematics, science and ICT but does not include the impact of arts and cultural experiences within a child's total education. It appears that this is due to an insufficient understanding of the implementation process.

This comprehensive investigation – by its very nature – revealed different findings. Educational systems are deeply embedded in cultural and nation specific contexts. This is especially the case as regards education in the arts. More than any other subject, the arts (itself a broad category) reflect unique cultural circumstances, and consequently, so does the teaching of the subject.

However, this caveat notwithstanding, it is possible to draw certain overall conclusions and to find common denominators, which can serve as guides for future reforms, changes and revisions of current programmes of arts education.

It imperative to note that arts education has impact on 1) the child; 2) the teaching and learning environment, and; on 3) the community.

Of most significance are the complementary but different benefits that accrue through education in the arts disciplines and those achieved through the use of artistic approaches to the teaching and learning of other discipline areas, in other words, education through the arts. This is an important finding as previous studies have tended to confuse these areas or see these two distinct areas as being one. It is essential to note, that for a children to maximise their educational potential, **both** approaches are needed. *Education in the arts* and *education through the arts*, while distinct, are interdependent and it should not be assumed that it is possible to adopt one or the other to achieve the totality of positive impacts on the child's educational realization.

Equally, it is of significance that high quality education where there is the greatest impact at all levels – child, learning environment and community – is achieved where excellent programmes exist both in the arts and through artistic approaches, such as in case study examples from Canada, Australia, United Kingdom, Finland, New Zealand, Slovakia and others.

Throughout the results of the survey there is an unequivocal indication that the positive benefits of arts-rich education only occur within the provision of quality programmes. The case studies and qualitative results contained within the compendium suggest that a quality arts programme includes the following characteristics:

- Active partnerships between schools and arts organisations and between teachers, artists and the community;
- Shared responsibility for planning, implementation and assessment and evaluation;
- Opportunities for public performance, exhibition and/or presentation;
- A combination of development within the specific art forms (education in the arts) with artistic and creative approaches to learning (education through the arts);
- Provision for critical reflection, problem solving and risk taking;
- Emphasis on collaboration;
- An inclusive stance with accessibility to all children;
- Detailed strategies for assessing and reporting on children's learning, experiences and development;
- Ongoing professional learning for teachers, artists and the community, and;
- Flexible school structures and permeable boundaries between schools and the community.

It is within the context of these quality programmes that the reports four major conclusions should be read. These are:

- There is a difference between, what can be termed, *education in the arts* (e.g. teaching in fine arts, music, drama, crafts, etc.) and *education through the arts* (e.g. the use of arts as a pedagogical tool in other subjects, such as numeracy, literacy and technology);
- Quality arts education tends to be characterised by a strong partnership between the schools and outside arts and community organisations. (In other words it is teachers, artists and the communities, which *together* share the responsibility for the delivery of the programmes);
- There is a need for more training for key providers at the coalface of the delivery-chain (e.g. teachers, artists, and other pedagogical staff), and;
- Quality arts education has distinct benefits for children in such areas as, among others, health and socio-cultural well-being.

As previously noted, definitions of arts education are varied and context specific. This, as has been shown in chapter 4, is so for a number of socio-economic reasons. Above all, inclusions within arts education vary according to the economic development of a country.

Yet, educational policies are not merely a consequence of economic development. Institutional factors also play a role. In some states the arts have traditionally relied on support from the public sector, in others less so. Hence funding for arts education funding is not limited to grants from public bodies, e.g. like ministries of education and culture, but come from a number of sources and partnerships (including from civil society). In short, not one but many different agencies – public as well as private and communal – support arts education.

This diversification of funding streams is not merely of theoretical interest. Rather given the role of these agencies, it means that the diversity of supporting agencies in arts education needs to be considered in policy implementation.

Needless to say, implementation of policies is of crucial importance. Without the delivery of programmes the whole case for policy making is void. However, too little focus has been made on this issue. The survey suggests that policy-makers have more or less uncritically adopted a top-down approach to policy implementation, i.e. have assumed that policies developed by the centre have been implemented by agencies (such as schools and other providers of arts education). This assumption, widespread though it is, has not yielded the expected results. As shown in chapter 4, the reality is that central government and schools are jointly responsible for education policy.

Studies of optimal delivery of public policies in other areas have shown that attempts to influence arts education policy need to be directed not merely at central government but also at decentralised authorities. The survey suggests that this too holds true for the area of arts education.

Policies are more effectively implemented if the service providers and the stakeholders are involved in the decision-making process (what is sometimes known as 'bottom-up' implementation). Such processes of consultation are rarely present in the surveyed countries; those responsible for the deliver of arts education have limited input into arts education policy (refer to chapters 4, 5 and 6 for details).

To remedy this implementation problem is of crucial importance for the improvement of the quality of the future arts education to establish an evidence-based methodology for successful delivery of arts education. Based on the verification evident in the research – and in consultation with best-practice models of implementation of other public policies – successful delivery of arts education would appear to hinge upon six factors:

1. **Clear and Consistent Objectives:** explicit goals for quality arts education – including both education in the arts and general education through artistic approaches – should provide standards for implementers, which increase the likelihood of successful implementation;

2. **Evidence Base/Adequate Causal Theory:** many arts education policies fail because they are based on flawed causal theories, which have not been tested independently in longitudinal programmes;
3. **Minimisation of veto-points:** A delivery chain, which reduced the risks of bureaucratic obstruction, resource limitations and stop-gaps;
4. **Committed and skilful implementation officers.** Efforts must be made to acknowledge the perspective of teachers, artists and the community, provide adequate teacher education and to structure delivery around the front-line staff;
5. **Consistent and Continuous Political Support:** arts education policies are more likely to be implemented if there is ongoing support – both tangible and intangible – for the value of education in and through the arts, and;
6. **Favourable External Conditions:** Absence of external conditions which can hamper implementation, e.g. budget cuts, recessions, lack of adequate time and resources etc.

However, this model is indicative only. Further research is required to test the applicability of this model across different cases, countries and cultures in arts education.

The overall rationale for arts education seems to have changed little over the years: cultural, social and aesthetic goals are the main reasons given for arts education. At a time when educational policies are often perceived to be output driven and focused on such skills as numeracy and literacy, it is perhaps not surprising that the arts are generally not viewed as being an important part of general education policy.

This lower priority of arts education has a number of implications. Unlike in numeracy and literacy, where the teachers have received specialist training, it is commonly the case that generalist teachers – with little or no arts education training – are responsible for teaching arts education. One might speculate that this lack of specialist training is one of the reasons why artists and the community are taking an increasing role in arts education.

Partnerships (with artists and cultural organisations) and experiences outside the classroom are, to be sure, a valuable part of quality arts education. Yet, community involvement in education is in it self desirable, yet it is not a substitute for formal qualifications, hence a review of the training in arts education is urgently needed.

It is impossible – on the basis of this survey – to determine why arts education seems to have been short-shifted by educational authorities. Arts education is universally part of the curriculum. Similarly, the results suggest that artistic approaches and arts-rich curricula enhance the quality of teaching and learning, both within the arts and across other disciplines (see chapter 7 for details). Yet, while arts education is part of education policy in practically all countries, there is considerable difference between what is mandated and the nature and quality of the arts education programme the children in schools actually receive. Most governments at least pay-lip service to engendering a culture in which arts-rich education can thrive, yet it is generally the case that there is a gap between espoused policy in arts education and typically poor provisions experienced within classrooms.

One of the reasons for this is that the effects of arts education, by and large, are based on anecdotal evidence but uncorroborated by empirical facts. Arts education is unlikely to be given a higher priority unless it can be established that provisions for this has tangible benefits.

To carry out this research is however, easier said than done. It is difficult – if not down-right impossible – to conclusively quantify the effect of arts education. To establish that arts education has a positive effect can not be done through statistical models alone. Such methodologies, while valuable, must be complemented with more ethnographic methods, like focus groups, interviews, observation, narrative and reflections (written and visual), in other words through what has sometimes been called 'thick description' methods (Geertz 1973).

Qualitative research models are not unique to arts education. Similar approaches have gained a foothold in management science. Traditional bastions of quantifiable approaches and statistical studies such as business schools and MBA programmes are now embracing cultural aspects of organisational lives. Myths, stories and folklore are used by management experts as much as numeric approaches in organisations that rely on results to predict future human actions and experiences. Such thorough qualitative research has not been forthcoming, reflecting the often explicit positivist preference in official education research. Greater research is needed on the impact of arts-rich programmes on general education if arts education is to be given a higher priority.

As noted previously, one of the most important distinctions revealed in the survey is between, *Education in the arts* and *Education through the arts*. The survey shows that the former is more likely at secondary level, while the latter, i.e. integrated education *through the arts* is more common at the elementary school level.

Especially the latter seems to be an area in which additional research is likely to reveal further benefits. The findings from the report (see chapter 7) clearly indicate that quality arts education programmes led to improvements in academic achievement. Art education is not only of intrinsic value for engendering human flourishing and critical self-esteem, it also has a positive impact on other aspects of learning. For example, 71% of countries felt that arts education had enhanced academic performance, especially in the areas of literacy and learning of languages. This effect occurred in quality programmes that included both education in the arts and education through artistic and creative approaches.

Moreover, arts education tends to lead to an improvement in student, parental and community perceptions of schools, as well as arts-rich programmes improving students' attitudes to school. Again these findings are not conclusive but they indicate that more longitudinal research is needed on the impact of arts education especially as regards the possible connections between arts education, cognitive development and health and well-being impacts for young people.

Arts education increases co-operation, respect, responsibility, tolerance, and appreciation, and has a positive impact on the development of social and cultural understanding. One of the reasons for this could be that arts-rich programmes appear to encourage more focused classroom interactions, greater concentration during school and more consistent school attendance- especially in boys and marginalised ('at-risk') students.

This effect also works the other way round, where poor quality arts education or no arts education may, in fact, inhibit the development of creativity and imagination. For instance, in 25% of countries the lack of arts education or the poor quality of programmes was seen to have had negative effects on the development of creativity and innovative thinking in youth.

Factors that were seen to be likely to limit the success of an arts programme were primarily a lack of time, space and resources. As noted previously, the ingenuity of teachers and artists to deliver effective programmes within a climate of severely limited resources was evident in many national examples. This should not be taken to mean that the arts should not be adequately resourced in terms of human and fiscal resources, time and facilities. The difficulty of juggling these issues was apparent in the *Poetry Ireland* project:

> The WIS has been delivering a high-quality and successful programme within severe funding limitations. The impact of fluctuation in funding to Poetry Ireland and the WIS staff changes has emerged in the data on participation and in the perception among some that the programme may have ceased. To an extent, this has undermined some of the progress and initiatives achieved.

> Uncertainty about the specific funding allocation each year causes great difficulty in planning; a long-term strategy incorporating a five-year development plan is not possible without multi-annual funding.

Allied to this, there was a general perception expressed that policy support for the arts within general education was not being translated into a strong push for increased arts resources at the coal face. In some countries the challenges facing education in general were so large that it became almost impossible to provide quality arts-rich provisions. For example, the problems of foreign debt, spiralling costs, low teacher salaries, and almost non-existent teaching and technical resources were seen to be major inhibiting factors in ensuring quality arts provisions within education in Kyrgyzstan. In this country there is strong commitment to the value of arts as shown through the promotion of arts education at a national level and the instigation of a number of laws covering *"Madaniat"* (culture) within education. Similarly, there has been a rapid increase in teacher education and arts provisions within further and higher education but the success of these initiatives have been tempered by the financial constraints.

For example, the Council of Europe noted that there was a "lack of commitment at an EU level to the value of arts education." Furthermore, even where policy support exists, implementation of programmes involving partnerships may be limited by organisational structures and the pragmatic difficulties of negotiated relationships between teachers and artists.

In Colombia, where there is strong support for the arts at a National level, the regional rollout of this policy has been more challenging, despite several very key examples of success within the regions. The Colombian response highlights the complications of effecting arts policy by stating that, "One of the great challenges for the implementation of the plan consists in the decentralization of the programme without losing unity and cohesion."

Within the curriculum, assessment and evaluation issues were seen to be particularly problematic. These aspects were often restrictive and did not account for the types of holistic and continuing learning common within arts programmes. In terms of evaluating the success or otherwise of a programme, many respondents reported the challenges of finding appropriate research, evaluation and analysis methodologies. Often the nature of the project design or government policy prescribed very quantitative methodology but this was challenging and generally not appropriate. It was noted that in recent times more qualitative approaches have been accepted and used for arts evaluation.

In Spain it was observed that "there continue to be lots of challenges including time, space, resources, finances, teacher issues, artist issues organisation and policy issues [and that] issues of research and evaluation are also important but we have little funds to gather this evidence." Similarly in Scotland it was reported that "Gaps in the available evidence, especially in relation to data collection methods, longitudinal studies and more research with under-represented groups" limited the ability to fully evaluate the impact of arts-based learning. Specifically, they called for more research "in relation to the role of creativity in education and problem solving, cognitive and social development."

The challenges of determining the impact that the arts have on students' learning appears to be a sustained area of concern inhibiting the further adoption of arts-rich education, as it was bemoaned in Nigeria:

> "Although the project was highly successful, how much of this success was due to the arts component or due to the structure of the program. Could the same results be derived with an after school sports or science or other programs that provided, transportation to and from, snacks, and caring interested adult supervision in a safe environment?"

Relationships with teachers and teacher capabilities were also raised as concerns that limit the wider adoption of arts-based pedagogy. As was noted extensively in chapter 5, teachers need the skills, attitudes and enthusiasm to drive arts-based programmes. While these can be nurtured through the course of successful programmes, it may take some time before teacher issues can be resolved within a given context. Canada made the specific call for "teacher education, especially for generalist teachers in elementary schools." The problem of teacher professional development is further compounded by a lack of financial and other resources.

While not specified within the report, several case studies eluded to 'Student issues' as being a limiting factor. It could be assumed that these refer to micro level issues related to students' participation in the programme and the interaction with staff involved in the programme. There also seemed to be some indication that student issues may refer to the manner in which students become empowered within the arts and the challenges this can cause for systems of education.

Almost every example of quality arts-rich education highlighted the importance of partnerships and the value of working closely with the local community. Clearly an ability to contextualise a programme to become a formative part of a local community was of worth. Yet this process was not without problems. Engendering of strong community participation and community recognition of arts-rich education were challenging things to achieve in practice and involved considerable negotiation, outreach and reinforcement. Once again, it was acknowledged that a lack of time, resources and the generally short-lived nature of many arts programmes hampered the possibility for greater connections to be forged with the community. Particularly in economically developing communities, the lack of perpetuation of projects and financial constraints meant that full community engagement and empowerment was unlikely.

Finally, in terms of limitations, rigid models of arts learning were seen to be problematic. It was suggested that arts education had failed to fully connect with contemporary learning issues and that this had caused it to be further distanced from core educational agendas. In Colombia it was noted that "Art education is not stagnate. The arts change as society changes, but by and large arts programmes have not. For arts education to yield optimal results, teachers need to embrace new technologies, e.g. in the form of training in ICT and professional skills relevant to the arts."

To conclude, the global research contained within this book underlines the importance of both education in and education through the arts in a range of contexts around the world. It emphasises that art education does not occurs as the result solely of policy or a mandate but rather as a complex web of social forces. To fully understand the way arts-rich curricula are enacted requires the study of the qualitative factors which influence why and how what occurs within schools is different from policy and espoused inclusion of the arts in education. Terms such as "culture", "creativity", "imagination" and so on appear frequently in policy documents but observations of teachers in action tend to reveal quite different dominant discourses.

The actions of an individual teacher, artist or member of the community delivering art education to children may be more closely effected by factors such as resources, diversity of pupils, socioeconomic location of the school, pressures on teachers, perceived values of the arts, educational authorities, pressures of assessment and the like. In arts education, policy is one thing, what children get delivered is another, but above all the ultimate focus must be on the meaning they construct from these experiences.

Early in life, children gain skills, knowledge and wisdom through an integrated process of learning that uses a range of aesthetic stimuli to enhance the learning process. For example, we sing to young children. We fill their environment with colourful and enticing imagery. Our voices and hand gestures take on distinctly dramatic and exaggerated forms when we talk to young children and parents often dance, clap and move their young children in rhythmic patterns. Universally we are applying the arts to enhance the child's learning processes. If you watch young children at play, you will see them naturally communicating in artistic forms.

Art allows us to ritualise and stylise aspects of our life making complexities understandable and easier to deal with. Art is a normal and necessary behaviour of human beings that like other common and universal occupations and preoccupations such as talking, working, exercising, socialising, learning, loving, caring and playing should be recognized, encouraged and developed in everyone. (Dissanayake 1999)

By the time young children enter school they are equipped with a range of artistic abilities and have used these creative processes to learn to walk, talk and play. Unfortunately, frequently the value of the arts as fundamental to human existence and learning is often overlooked in formal education situations. Too often instead of receiving an arts-rich education, the majority of children experience an art-starved educational experience.

Learning democracy. Storytelling workshop through intimate everyday objects to launch a one-year inter-disciplinary cultural literacy school project which culminated in the collective mosaic Land is Life (4m x 6m, Santa Catarina, Brazil 2003). Photo courtesy of Dan Baron Cohen.

In too many instances, the arts are kept as a token activity for the annual school concert or as something to use up 30 minutes of time on a Friday afternoon. Even things such as lunchtime band, choir, dance or craft clubs – while often in themselves a positive experience – do not constitute adequate arts experiences for children. By the time the child enters secondary school, the arts tend to be separated from the mainstream curriculum and students undertake the arts – if at all – in isolated lessons or courses, often given as electives, rather than being central to the core processes of learning.

The results of the research indicate that all societies in the world engage actively in the arts and that most countries value the arts – at least value it in terms of the rhetoric – within education policy. The world is currently in a time where the arts are flourishing within the commercial, consumer and social sectors. Contemporary communication abounds with arts content in terms of images, sound and action. Modern society is witnessing the enormous growth in the innovative, consumer-driven 'creative industries' sectors. Humans have evolved to be 'arts-inclined' individuals.

Given the view that the arts are a core aspect of current and future human existence, it seems hardly surprising that when school environments are deprived of the arts, learning and social development is hindered. In the 1980s, many school districts in the United States of America opted to reduce the arts within the school curriculum. It was considered that the arts were an 'optional extra' that under economic rationalist models of education could be removed. The impact of removing the arts from the curriculum was felt almost immediately. Academic performance suffered and the social cohesion, cooperation and balance within school communities were negatively affected. Teachers and students missed the arts, and by the early 1990s a concerted effort was made to reinstate the arts within schools and to assert the centrality of the arts within quality democratic education.

Ernest L. Boyer, president of the Carnegie Foundation for the Advancement of Teaching argues that "During the past quarter century, literally thousands of school-based programmes have demonstrated beyond question that the arts can not only bring coherence to our fragmented academic world, but through the arts, students' performance in other academic disciplines can be enhanced as well." (Boyer 1987)

It has been said often that traditional schooling fails to meet the needs of many children who are marginalised within the education systems and that the arts may serve to redress this concern. Sometimes, the student who is not doing well in traditional academics might have an artistic talent that has not yet flowered. As the writers of "The Fourth R" point out: "Imagine what might happen to Leonardo da Vinci today if he were placed in the average public school. This illegitimate son of a poor woman, a left-handed writer who loved to draw and challenge conventional thought, would be labelled an at-risk special education candidate..." Schools with an integrated arts curriculum might be better able to address the needs of students like Leonardo.

In recent years, there has been increasing interest in the potential of arts-based educational programmes to enhance the learning outcomes. However, to date there has been only limited attempts to collate and analyse rigorous research that examines either the process or the outcomes of the use of such programmes. Despite the difficulties of developing a research methodology that allows for the gathering of what could be considered "hard evidence" of impact and implementation strategies, the extensive body of evidence contributed to the global study underpinning the analysis in this book bears testament to the value and importance of the arts within general education provisions.

It is hoped that the analysis contained within this book will serve to activate policy makers, teachers, artists and parents to develop, implement and value art-rich education for all children. Quality arts education programmes have an impact on the child; the teaching and learning environment, and; on the community, but these benefits only exist where quality programmes are in place. Poor quality and inadequate programmes do little to enhance the educational potential of the child or build first-rate schools. It is important that the rhetoric of policy that supports the inclusion of arts education within the total educational experiences of the child is backed by substantial implementation and monitoring structures that ensures children receive high quality programmes. These programmes are no more expensive to implement than poor quality programmes and afford the opportunity to initiate sustained educational reform and greatly enhance the overall excellence of education.

Education should be centred on the *Wow factor* engendered through the arts and build in all young people innovation minds, a creative spirits and an enthusiasm for life and learning.

References

Arendt, H. (1958). *The Human Condition.* Chicago, University of Chicago Press.

Arendt, H. (1983). *Between Past and Future.* London, Penguin.

Aristotle (1965). On the Art of Poetry. *Aristotle, Horace, Longinus: Classical Literary Criticism.* D. T.S. London, Penguin.

Ashton, L. (1998). *I can't draw to save myself.* Australian Institute of Art Education, University of Wollongong.

Ashton, L. (1999). "Deconstructing the aesthetic discourse of drawing: A study of generalist primary teachers in transition." *Australian Art Education* 22(2): 41-61.

Benjamin, W. (1996). *Illuminations.* London, Pimlico.

Boughton, D. (1999). "How to build an art teacher (1986)." *Australian Art Education* 22(1): 59-67.

Boyer, E. (1987). *College: The undergraduate experience in America.* New York, Harper and Row.

Brady, L., G. Segal, et al. (1998). "Student perceptions of the theory and practice nexus in teacher education." *Educational Practice and Theory into Practice* 20(1): 5-16.

Bresler, L. (1995). "American arts education in elementary schools: Craft, child art and fine art." *INSEA News* 2(1): 7-10

Carroll, K. L. (1997). Researching paradigms in art education. *Research methods and methodologies for art education.* S. La Pierre, D. and E. Zimmerman. Reston, Virginia, The National Art Education Association: 171-192.

Cassirer, E. (1974). *An essay on man: an introduction to philosophy of human culture.* New Haven, Yale University Press.

Chalmers, F. G. (1998). "Teaching drawing in nineteenth-century Canada – Why?" *Curriculum, culture and art education: comparative perspectives.* K. Freedman and F. Hernandez. New York, State University of New York Press.

Chia, J., J. Matthews, et al. (1995). "A window on an art classroom." *INSEA News* 2(1): 4-7.

Cizek, F. (1921). *The child as artist: Some conversations with Professor Cizek.* Knightsbridge, England, Children's Art Exhibition Fund.

Condous, J. (1999). "How well are the arts in education taught? (1979)." *Australian Art Education* 22(1): 15-21.

Cunliffe, L. (1990). "Tradition, mediation and growth in art education." *Journal of Art and Design Education* 9(3): 271-288.

Cunneen, C. and R. White (1995). *Juvenile Justice – an Australian perspective.* Melbourne, Australia, Oxford University Press.

Dahllof, U., J. Harris, et al. (1991). *Dimensions of evaluation: Report of the IMHE study group on evaluation in higher education.* London, Jessica Kingsley Publishers.

Dewey, J. (1934). *Art as experience.* New York, Minton Balch.

Diamond, P. C. T. and C. A. Mullen (1999). *The Post-modern Educator: Arts-based inquiries and teacher development.* New York, Peter Lang.

Disch, L. J. (1996). "More truth than fact: Storytelling as critical understanding in the writings of Hannah Arendt." *Political Theory* 21(4): 665-694.

Dissanayake, E. (1999). *Homo Aestheticus: Where art comes from and why.* Seattle, The Free Press.

Duncum, P. (1999). "Primary art pedagogy: Everything a generalist teacher needs to know." *Australian Art Education* 21(3): 15-23.

Eisner, E. (1991). *The enlightened eye*. New York, McMillan.

Eisner, E. (1997). "The state of art education today and some potential remedies: A report to the national endowment for the arts." *Art Education* **50**(1): 27-28, 61-72.

Eisner, E. (1999). "The national assessment in the visual arts." *Art Education Policy Review* **100**(6): 16-19.

Ellis, C. (1954). Preparing art educators. *Education and Art: A symposium*. E. Ziegfeld. Paris, UNESCO.

Emery, L. (1999). "13 Years on ... a response to Boughton." *Australian Art Education* **22**(1): 68-70.

Errazuriz, L. (1998). Rationales for art education in Chilean schools. *Curriculum, culture and art education: comparative perspectives*. K. Freedman and F. Hernandez. New York, State University of New York Press.

Foster, H., Ed. (1983). *The anti-aesthetic: Essays on postmodern culture*, Bay Press.

Foucault, M. (1998). *Aesthetic, method and epistemology*. New York, New Press.

Freedman, K. (1998). "Sharing interests: aesthetics, technology and visual culture in democratic education." *Australian Art Education* **21**(2): 3-10.

Freedman, K. and F. Hernandez, Eds. (1998). *Curriculum, culture and art education: Contemporary perspectives*. New York, State University of New York Press.

Geahigan, G. (1999). "Teaching preservice art education majors: "The world of the work"." *Art Education* **52**(5): 12-17.

Geertz, C. (1973). *The Interpretation of Cultures*. Princeton, Princeton University Press.

Greer, D., W. (1992). "Harry Broudy and Disciplined-Based Art Education (DBAE)." *Journal of Aesthetic Education* **26**(4): 49-60.

Guba, E. G. and Y. Lincoln, S. (1989). *Fourth generation evaluation*. London, Sage publications.

Hernandez, F. (1998). Framing the empty space: Two examples of the history of art education in the Spanish political context. *Curriculum, culture and art education: comparative perspectives*. K. Freedman and F. Hernandez. New York, State University of New York Press.

Holt, D., Ed. (1997). *Primary arts education: Contemporary issues*. London, The Falmer Press.

Jones, J. (1998). *The Role of the EAP Within the Juvenile Justice System*. International Forum on Education in Penal Systems, Conference Proceedings, Youth Research Centre, University of Melbourne, Australia.

Keifer-Boyd, K. (1996). "Interfacing hypermedia and the internet with critical inquiry in the arts: preservice training in art education." *Art Education* **49**(6): 33-41.

Keifer-Boyd, K. (1997). "Interfacing hypermedia and the internet with critical inquiry in the arts: Preservice training." *New technologies and art education: implications for theory, research and practice*. D. Gregory, C. Reston, Virginia, The National Art Education Association: 23-33.

Kissick, J. (1993). *Art: Context and criticism*. Bristol, Wm C. Brown Communications, Inc.

Kvale, S. (1994). *Validation as communication and action: On the social construction of validity*. Postmodernist Approaches to validity in Qualitative Research, American Educational Research Association Conference., New Orleans, ED 371 020.

Langer, S., K. (1957). *Problems of Art*. London, Routledge and Kegan Paul.

Levi-Strauss, C. (1966). *The Savage Mind (Nature of Human Society)*. Chicago, University of Chicago Press.

Lincoln, Y., S. and E. Guba, G. (1988). *Criteria for assessing naturalistic inquiries as reports*. The Annual Meeting of the American Educational Research Association. New Orleans, ED 297007.

Lovgren, S. and K. Sten-Gosta (1998). "From art making to visual communication: Swedish art education in the twentieth century." *Curriculum, culture and art education: comparative perspectives*. K. Freedman and F. Hernandez. New York, State University of New York Press.

Lowenfeld, V. and L. Brittain, W. (1964). *Creative and mental growth*. New York, Macmillan.

May, W. T. (1993). *Art experts' views of an ideal curriculum*. Elementary Subjects Center. Series No. 95. East Lansing, Center for the Learning and Teaching of Elementary Subjects: 1-156.

Nakamura, K. (1999). "Pre-service teachers' art appreciation." *INSEA News* 5(3): 10-11.

Parmenter, C. (1995). "A classroom in Oz." *INSEA News* 2(1): 8.

Pearsall, J., Ed. (1998). *The New Oxford Dictionary of English*. Oxford, Claredon Press.

Piaget, J. (1954). "Art education and child psychology." *Education and Art: A symposium*. E. Ziegfeld. Paris, UNESCO.

Read, H. (1970). *The redemption of the robot: My encounter with education through art*. London, Faber.

Richardson, D. (1999). "The concept of "art"." *Australian Art Education* 21(3): 24-27.

Richardson, M. (1948). *Art and the child*. London, University of London Press.

Schrag, P. (1999). *Paradise Lost: California's Experience America's Future*. Berkeley, University of California Press.

Smith, J., K. (1993). *After the demise of empiricism: The problem of judging social and educational inquiry*. Norwood, New Jersey, Ablex Publishing Corporation.

Smith, R. (1995). "The question of modernism and postmodernism." *Art Education Policy Review* 96(6): 2-11.

Taylor, R. (1986). *Educating for critical response and development*. London, Longman.

Thistlewood, D. (1998). "From imperialism to internationalism: Policy making in British art education." *Curriculum, culture and art education: comparative perspectives*. K. Freedman and F. Hernandez. New York, State University of New York Press.

Wilson, B. (1997). "The second search: Metaphor, dimensions of meaning, and research topics in art education." *Research methods and methodologies for art education*. S. La Pierre, D. and E. Zimmerman. Reston, Virginia, The National Art Education Association: 1-32.

Wilson, B. (1999). "The Success and failure of art education: Assessing the results (1976)." *Australian Art Education* 22(1): 2-7.

Wright, S. (1989). "We've got it backwards: It's too late by age 8." *Australian Art Education* 13(1): 6-10.

Zimmerman, E. (1994). "Concerns of pre-service art teachers and those who prepare them to teach." *Art Education* 47(5): 59-67.

Index

Appendix One: Copy of survey

Name:	
Position:	
Organisation:	
Country:	

1. **Please cross one or more boxes if the following subjects are included in Arts Education in your country:**

   Performance art   ☐

   Film and Media   ☐

   Dance   ☐

   Drama   ☐

   Music   ☐

   Painting   ☐

   Sculpture   ☐

   Digital art   ☐

   Drawing   ☐

   Craft   ☐

   Design   ☐

   Painting   ☐

   Sculpture   ☐

   Other(s) <please specify>   ☐ _____

On average how many minutes per week are devoted to arts education in:

Primary/elementary Schools   _____

Secondary Schools   _____

Please write additional comments

_____

_____

_____

_____

_____

Please respond to the following general questions, answering yes/no/don't know

2. **Arts Education is a Mandated/Compulsory part of the curriculum**

   Yes ☐   No ☐   Don't Know ☐

3. **Arts Education is a freestanding subject (like literacy and mathematics):**

   Yes ☐   No ☐   Don't Know ☐

4. **Arts Education is an examined part of the curriculum**

   Yes ☐   No ☐   Don't Know ☐

5. **Please cross one or more boxes if the following goals influence Arts Education in your country:**

   Artistic/aesthetic goals   ☐
   Social goals   ☐
   Cultural goals   ☐
   Economic goals   ☐
   Literacy goals   ☐
   Numeracy goals   ☐
   Personal goals   ☐
   Other(s) <please specify>   ☐ _____

6. **Please cross one or more boxes indicating who is responsible for Arts Education policy:**

   Central government   ☐
   State or provincial government   ☐
   Local education authorities   ☐
   School based decisions   ☐
   Parents   ☐
   Children   ☐
   Artists   ☐
   Teachers   ☐
   Community   ☐
   Other(s) <please specify>   ☐ _____

7. **Please cross one or more boxes indicating who is responsible for teaching Arts Education and the amount of training they receive.**

Amount of arts education training received

Parents	☐ none	☐ less than 3 months	☐ 3-12 months	☐ more than 1 year
Generalist Teachers	☐ none	☐ less than 3 months	☐ 3-12 months	☐ more than 1 year
Artists	☐ none	☐ less than 3 months	☐ 3-12 months	☐ more than 1 year
Specialist Teachers	☐ none	☐ less than 3 months	☐ 3-12 months	☐ more than 1 year
Community	☐ none	☐ less than 3 months	☐ 3-12 months	☐ more than 1 year
Other <specify below>	☐ none	☐ less than 3 months	☐ 3-12 months	☐ more than 1 year

Other(s) _____

Please respond to the following questions indicating

Strongly Agree	☐
Agree	☐
Don't Know	☐
Disagree	☐
Strongly Disagree	☐

(Please write examples in the space provided)

8. **Arts education project(s) in your country have contributed to improved student artistic achievement**

Strongly Agree	☐
Agree	☐
Don't Know	☐
Disagree	☐
Strongly Disagree	☐

Please give examples

_____
_____
_____
_____
_____

9. **Arts education project(s) in your country have contributed to improved levels of educational attainment/academic improvement:**

Strongly Agree   ☐
Agree   ☐
Don't Know   ☐
Disagree   ☐
Strongly Disagree   ☐

Please give examples

_____

_____

_____

_____

_____

10. **Arts education project(s) in your country have contributed to improved student attitude:**

Strongly Agree   ☐
Agree   ☐
Don't Know   ☐
Disagree   ☐
Strongly Disagree   ☐

Please give examples

_____

_____

_____

_____

_____

11. **Arts education project(s) in your country have contributed to improved student confidence:**

Strongly Agree   ☐
Agree   ☐
Don't Know   ☐
Disagree   ☐
Strongly Disagree   ☐

Please give examples

_____

_____

_____

_____

_____

12. Arts education project(s) in your country have contributed to student social/cultural development:

Strongly Agree ☐
Agree ☐
Don't Know ☐
Disagree ☐
Strongly Disagree ☐

Please give examples

_____

_____

_____

_____

_____

13. Arts education project(s) in your country have contributed to teacher professional development:

Strongly Agree ☐
Agree ☐
Don't Know ☐
Disagree ☐
Strongly Disagree ☐

Please give examples

_____

_____

_____

_____

_____

14. Arts education project(s) in your country have contributed to positive changes in arts policy:

Strongly Agree ☐
Agree ☐
Don't Know ☐
Disagree ☐
Strongly Disagree ☐

Please give examples

_____
_____
_____
_____
_____

15. Arts education project(s) in your country have contributed to positive changes in education policy:

Strongly Agree ☐
Agree ☐
Don't Know ☐
Disagree ☐
Strongly Disagree ☐

Please give examples

_____
_____
_____
_____
_____

16. Arts education project(s) in your country have contributed to more family and community involvement in arts and/or education:

Strongly Agree ☐
Agree ☐
Don't Know ☐
Disagree ☐
Strongly Disagree ☐

Please give examples

_____

_____

_____

_____

_____

17. Arts education has improved the mental or physical health of individuals:

Strongly Agree   ☐

Agree   ☐

Don't Know   ☐

Disagree   ☐

Strongly Disagree   ☐

Please give examples

_____

_____

_____

_____

_____

18. Arts Education has contributed to teaching creativity:

Strongly Agree   ☐

Agree   ☐

Don't Know   ☐

Disagree   ☐

Strongly Disagree   ☐

Please give examples

_____

_____

_____

_____

_____

19. Arts Education has contributed to teaching imagination:

Strongly Agree   ☐
Agree   ☐
Don't Know   ☐
Disagree   ☐
Strongly Disagree   ☐

Please give examples

_____

_____

_____

_____

20. Arts Education has contributed to teaching manual abilities:

Strongly Agree   ☐
Agree   ☐
Don't Know   ☐
Disagree   ☐
Strongly Disagree   ☐

Please give examples

_____

_____

_____

_____

21. Arts Education has contributed to teaching concentration:

Strongly Agree   ☐
Agree   ☐
Don't Know   ☐
Disagree   ☐
Strongly Disagree   ☐

Please give examples

_____

_____

_____

_____

22. Arts Education has contributed to teaching information and communications technologies (ICT), computer skills and technology skills:

Strongly Agree   ☐
Agree   ☐
Don't Know   ☐
Disagree   ☐
Strongly Disagree   ☐

Please give examples

_____

_____

_____

_____

23. Arts Education has contributed to improved community ties/bonds:

Strongly Agree   ☐
Agree   ☐
Don't Know   ☐
Disagree   ☐
Strongly Disagree   ☐

Please give examples

_____

_____

_____

_____

_____

24. Arts Education has contributed to improved the dialogue between different cultures and improved understanding of others' cultures:

Strongly Agree   ☐
Agree   ☐
Don't Know   ☐
Disagree   ☐
Strongly Disagree   ☐

Please give examples

_____

_____

_____

_____

_____

Please cross one or more boxes if arts education has benefited from the involvement (financial or otherwise) of the following institutions/groups/organizations:

Churches/religious organizations	☐
Central Government	☐
Industry	☐
Galleries	☐
International organizations	☐
Broadcasters	☐
Foundations/charities	☐
Individuals	☐
Trade Unions	☐

Please provide examples

_____

_____

_____

_____

_____

NEXT...Please complete the following Case Study section(s).

Case Study 1

Please select a research project (or projects, to a maximum of three per country) that has been conducted in your country that:

- Involves the arts in an educational context
- Addresses the needs of all children and young people with particular attention to educationally marginalised children and/or young people
- Has had an impact at a local and/or national level

1. **Provide the following information in relation to <u>each</u> selected project: Three forms are provided with this survey.**

Chief investigator(s) and/or investigation team:	<given name> <middle name> <family name>
Contact details:	Organization Address Country Phone email Website
Name of the project:	
Project aim(s):	
Description of the project:	(Less than 500 words)

2. What do you consider to be the main impact of the project on:

Note: If there was not an impact on one (or more) of these areas, leave that area blank

Government (local/federal/national and/or other)?	
Curricula/arts and/or education policy/ or other policy changes (local/federal/national and/or other)?	
Community (local/federal/national and/or other)?	
Teachers?	
Children and/or young people?	
Parents, carers and the family?	
Artists and/or performers?	
Other?	

3. How useful would you rate each of these research methods/measures/strategies in determining the impact of the project.

Circle the number on the scale that indicates usefulness

	Not useful								Most useful	
Interview	1	2	3	4	5	6	7	8	9	10
Questionnaire	1	2	3	4	5	6	7	8	9	10
Survey	1	2	3	4	5	6	7	8	9	10
Focus groups	1	2	3	4	5	6	7	8	9	10
Action research	1	2	3	4	5	6	7	8	9	10
Case study	1	2	3	4	5	6	7	8	9	10
Video/film	1	2	3	4	5	6	7	8	9	10
Stories/narrative	1	2	3	4	5	6	7	8	9	10
Photographs	1	2	3	4	5	6	7	8	9	10
Journals	1	2	3	4	5	6	7	8	9	10
Other (please specify)	1	2	3	4	5	6	7	8	9	10

4. What do you consider to be the main achievements of the project?

5. What do you consider to be the main challenges/issues/concerns of the project? Circle the number on the scale that indicates usefulness

	Not a problem							Most challenge		
Time	1	2	3	4	5	6	7	8	9	10
Space	1	2	3	4	5	6	7	8	9	10
Resources	1	2	3	4	5	6	7	8	9	10
Finances	1	2	3	4	5	6	7	8	9	10
Community participation	1	2	3	4	5	6	7	8	9	10
Community recognition	1	2	3	4	5	6	7	8	9	10
Student issues	1	2	3	4	5	6	7	8	9	10
Teacher issues	1	2	3	4	5	6	7	8	9	10
Artist issues	1	2	3	4	5	6	7	8	9	10
Organization or policy issues	1	2	3	4	5	6	7	8	9	10
Assessment/evaluation issues	1	2	3	4	5	6	7	8	9	10
Other (please specify)	1	2	3	4	5	6	7	8	9	10

Comments:

Any other comments:

7. Optional:

Attach three j-peg images of some aspect of the project. Ensure that any images that you provide have been approved for print and distribution.

Thank you for your valuable contributions to understanding arts education around the world.

Appendix Two: List of responding countries, ministries and/or organisations

International/trans-national	• International Federation of Arts Councils & Cultural Agencies • European Network of Cultural Administration Training Centres (ENCATC) • UNESCO • Observatory of Cultural Policies in Africa • European League of Institutes of the Arts • European Network of Art Organisations for Children and Young People • Council of Europe: *Culture, Creativity and the Young Project*
Argentina	• Observatorio Cultural • Cinema and Marginalised Children and Young People
Australia	• Australia Council • de Lissa Institute of Early Childhood & Family Studies Research Group (UniSA) • Queensland University of Technology • Murdoch University • National Affiliation of Arts Educators • University of Technology Sydney • University of Sydney • Victorian Department of Education and Training • Music for Learning for Life • Evaluation of School-based Arts Programmes in Australian Schools • ARTPLAY and Youth Programmes • Charles Darwin University • Northern Territory Department of Employment Education and Training • Queensland Performing Arts Centre • Sydney Opera House • Children's Voices
Austria	• Educult Institute for the Mediation of Arts and Science • Kulturkontakt Austria • Dance out of Line
Barbados	• Ministry of Education Youth Affairs and Sports
Belgium	• European Network of Cultural Administration Training Centres (ENCATC) • Ministry of the French Community
Bulgaria	• Policies for Culture

Canada	• Canada Council for the Arts • Center for Intercultural and Social Development • University of Toronto • Learning through the Arts • National Arts & Youth Demonstration Project, Mc Gill University • Coalition for Arts Education
Chile	• Consejo Nacional de la Cultura y las Artes • Ministerio de Educación de Chile
China	• Hong Kong Institute of Education • Arts-in-Education programme • The Arts-in-Education Programme (funded by the Hong Kong Bank Foundation)
Colombia	• Ministry of Culture • Plan Nacional de Música Para la Convivencia (National Programme of Music for Peaceful Coexistence) • Artistic and cultural school in the Norte of Santander
Czech Republic	• Ministry of Culture
Ecuador	• Ministry of Culture
England	• Arts Council England • Arts and Education Interface • Isaacs UK • Artsmark Impact Research Study • National Evaluation of Creative Partnerships
Finland	• Helsinki Polytechnic and Finnish Drama and Theatre Education Association • Ministry of Education • Girls, boys and 'gender play' • FAME – Forum for Alternative Methods in Education
France	• Ministry of Culture and Communication • "Windows opened to arts" ("Fenêtres sur Arts")
Germany	• Federation of Associations for Cultural Youth Education • Contemporary Dance School Hamburg • ERICarts
Guyana	• Ministry of Culture, Youth and Sport
India	• India Foundation for the Arts
Ireland	• The Arts Council of Ireland
Malaysia	• Arts Education Program for Young People • Arts Education Working Committee

Mongolia	• Ministry of Education, Culture and Science • Arts Council of Mongolia
Mozambique	• Observatory of Cultural Policies in Africa
New Zealand	• Ministry of Education • Creative New Zealand • Ministry for Culture and Heritage
Nigeria	• Ministry of Education • Royal Arcade • Tysog Ventures
Palau	• Belau National Museum
Peru	• Ministry of Education • International Issues Consultant
Republic of Congo	• SOCODIC
Scotland	• Scottish Arts Council • A Literature Review of the Evidence Base for Culture the Arts and Sport Policy
Senegal	• Inspecteur de l'Education artistique • The Empire of Children • The 'Educ' Art' School Carnival • BARGNY ART– SUR – MER workshops
Seychelles	• National Arts Council
Singapore	• National Arts Council
Slovakia	• Ministry of Education • Project of experimental verification of provisional curricula – art teaching – at primary school levels 1 and 2 • Tuition plans – extended aesthetics teaching for primary arts schools.
Spain	• Asociación Española para el Desarrollo del Mecenazgo Empresarial • Cultur Habeo • Open to Dawn
Sweden	• Ministry of Culture
Tanzania	• Tanzania Culture Trust Fund
The Netherlands	• European League of Institutes of the Arts • European Network of Art Organisations for Children and Young People • Netherlands Expertise Centre for Arts and Cultural Education • CKV1 (Arts and Cultural Education1)

United States of America (USA)	• Department of Education • Arts Education Partnership • Arts Partnerships in Education • Center for Arts and Culture • National Assembly of State Arts Agencies • Defining Proficiency in the Arts
Wales	• Arts Council of Wales • University of Wales Institute

Appendix Three: Research case study titles listed by country (these are in addition to the surveys and research listed in Appendix 2)

Full research details, particulars of commissioning and leading organisations and summaries of each of these case studies is available through the UNESCO website http://unesco.org/culture/lea

International/ transnational	• European Network of Art Organisations for Children and Youth • Culture, Creativity and the Young Project
Argentina	• Cinema and Marginalised Children and Young People
Australia	• Evaluation of School-based Arts programmes in Australian Schools • Music for Learning for life • Education and Arts Partnership Initiative (EAPI) • Children's voices
Austria	• Dance out of the Line
Barbados	• PEACE Programme
Brazil	• *Projecto Presente*
Canada	• National Arts and Youth Demonstration Project • Learning Through the Arts • Coalition for Arts Education
China	• Arts-in-Education Programme
Colombia	• *Plan Nacional de Musica Para la Convivencia* (National Programme of Music for Peaceful Coexistence) • *Formación Artistica en Danza a Niños y Jóvenes Vallecuacanos* • Artistic and cultural schools in the *Norte de Santander*
England	• Creative Partnerships • Artsmark • Arts and Education Interface: A mutual learning triangle?
Finland	• *FAME:* Forum for Alternative Activating Methods. • The Oak of Finland: Cultural Heritage Project • Gender Construction in the Context of School Art Education • Theatre and Drama in Grades 7-9 of Finnish Comprehensive Schools
France	• *Fenêtres sur Arts* (Windows opened to arts)
Malaysia	• *Anak Anak Kota* ("Children of the sun")

New Zealand	• Like Writing off the Paper: Report on student learning in the arts • An evaluation of the professional development to support the Arts in the New Zealand Curriculum. • The impact of facilitation on teaching and learning in the arts
Nigeria	• (National Study of) Secondary School Fine Arts Curriculum • Problems inherent in the implementation of secondary school fine arts curriculum and suggested solutions.
Republic of Ireland	• Artformations • Poetry Ireland: Writers in Schools Scheme • Learning outcomes in arts-in-education projects • Vogler Quartet in Sligo Residency Project
Scotland	• Evidence Base for Culture the Arts and Sport Policy
Senegal	• *Le Carnaval Scolaire:* The 'Educ'Art' School Carnival: The *Talibé,* a plea for difficult childhood • *L'Empire des enfants* (The Empire of Children) • *BARGNY ART – SUR – MER* Workshops.
Singapore	• Drama and Oral Language: An Investigation of the impact of process drama on the oral communication of NT4 students.
Slovakia	• Project of Experimental Verification of Provisional Curriculum-Art teaching at primary levels 1 and 2. • Tuition plans – extended aesthetics teaching for primary arts schools.
Spain	• Open to the Dawn
The Netherlands	• CKV1: Arts and Cultural Education 1 Monitoring Project
United Kingdom	• Artsmark Impact • Arts and Education Interface • Creative Partnerships
United States of America (USA)	• Arts Education in Public Elementary and Secondary Schools • How Arts Integration Supports Student Learning: Students Shed Light on the Connections • Chicago Arts Partners in Education • Defining Proficiency in the Arts

Appendix Four: Other countries also consulted (not survey respondents)

- Afghanistan
- Bangladesh
- Bhutan
- Brazil
- Cambodia
- Cook Islands
- Denmark
- Fiji
- Japan
- Jordan
- Kyrgyzstan
- Maldives
- Namibia
- Nepal
- Thailand
- Tonga
- Tuvalu

Waxmann

European Studies in Education
edited by Christoph Wulf

Aesthetic experience, in which the boundaries between outside and inside dissolve and the aesthetic object and subject become interlaced, is central to aesthetic education. On this basis, the point is to give children and adolescents, within a sphere of action characterised by tensions and contradictory demands, the possibility of developing a kind of "aesthetic wilfulness" as a capacity for self-development and self-determination.

■ Volume 24

Yasuo Imai,
Christoph Wulf (Eds.)

Concepts of Aesthetic Education
Japanese and European Perspectives

2007, 198 pages, pb., € 19,90
ISBN 978-3-8309-1761-8

The book assumes that mimetic, poietic, and performative ways of world making play an essential role in education. Any given culture and society can be analyzed as how these different ways of world making are interconnected. In educational processes there is an overlap of mimetic, poietic, and performative ways of world making, which often can only be analytically differentiated. These ways of world making do not conceive human practices as instances of rules or laws; the individual is represented not as rule-following, but as rule-producing. This position is at the core critical of rationality, without however surrendering the claim of reason to the irrational.

■ Volume 25

Shoko Suzuki,
Christoph Wulf (Eds.)

Mimesis, Poiesis, and Performativity in Education

2007, 232 pages, pb., € 19,90
ISBN 978-3-8309-1921-6

MÜNSTER · NEW YORK · MÜNCHEN · BERLIN